Name That MOVIE!

A PAINLESS VOCABULARY BUILDER

Watch Movies and Ace the
*SAT, ACT®, GED®, and GRE®!

Brian Leaf, M.A.

WILEY

Wiley Publishing, Inc.

Library of Congress Cataloging-in-Publication Data:
Leaf, Brian.
 Name that movie! : a painless vocabulary builder : romantic comedy and drama edition : watch movies and ace the SAT, ACT, GED and GRE! / Brian Leaf.
  p. cm.
  ISBN 978-0-470-90326-1 (pbk.)
  ISBN 978-0-470-94619-0 (ebk.)
 1. Vocabulary—Study guides. 2. English language—Glossaries, vocabularies, etc. 3. Educational tests and measurements—Study guides. 4. Comedy films—Quotations, maxims, etc. 5. Motion pictures—Quotations, maxims, etc. I. Title.
 PE1449.L327 2011
 428.1'076—dc22
                              2010039044

Printed in the United States of America

10 9 8 7 6 5 4 3 2 1

Book production by Wiley Publishing, Inc., Composition Services

Acknowledgments

Thanks to my agents, Todd Shuster and Colleen Rafferty, and my fantastic editors at Wiley, Greg Tubach and Carol Pogoni. Thanks to Amy Sell and Adrienne Fontaine at Wiley for getting the word out. Thanks to Pam Weber-Leaf for great editing tips, Zach Nelson for sage marketing advice, Ian Curtis for assiduous proofreading, Manny and Susan Leaf for everything, and of course, thanks most of all to Gwen, Noah, and Benjamin for love, support, and inspiration.

About the Author

Brian Leaf, M.A., is the author of the four-book *Defining Twilight* vocabulary workbook series as well as the four-book SAT and ACT test-prep series *McGraw-Hill's Top 50 Skills for a Top Score*. He is Director of the New Leaf Learning Center in Massachusetts, and has provided SAT, ACT, GED, SSAT, and GRE preparation to thousands of students throughout the United States. For more information, visit his Web site at www.brianleaf.com.

How to Use This Book

This book contains 100 excerpts from romantic comedy or drama movies. For each excerpt, see if you can name the movie, describe the scene(s), and define the boldfaced vocabulary words. If you need help naming a movie, check the hint at the bottom of the page. Then check your answers against the definitions provided in this book. To help you memorize new words in each group, copy or say each vocabulary word and its synonyms five times and reread the movie excerpt. Also, after every ten groups, take the two-page quiz that tests definitions, synonyms, and even word parts that you've learned. There's no easier or more fun way to learn more than 1,000 words for the SAT, ACT, GED, or GRE. By the end of this book, your vocabulary will be larger, your test scores will be higher, and you'll be a *Superbad* vocabulary scholar!

Group 1

Here's an excerpt from a movie. See if you can name the movie, describe the scene, and define the boldface vocabulary words. Check your answers on the following page.

E.C.: Uh, yes, Mr. Berty. Um . . . (*begins reciting lines from Romeo and Juliet*) "O, here will I set up my **everlasting** rest, and shake the **yoke** of **inauspicious** stars from this world-wearied flesh. Eyes, look your last! Arms, take your last embrace! and, lips, O you the doors of breath, seal with a **righteous** kiss a dateless bargain to **engrossing** death!"

Movie: _____

Scene: _____

_____

Everlasting might mean _____

_____

Yoke might mean _____

_____

Inauspicious might mean _____

_____

Righteous might mean _____

_____

Engrossing might mean _____

_____

Hint: "Now, who would like to repeat the last few lines of **iambic pentameter** just to show they were paying attention? Mr. Cullen?"

Solutions

Let's see how you did. Check your answers and write the exact definitions. To help you memorize the vocabulary words, reread the movie excerpt or even act out the scene with a friend.

Movie: *The Twilight Saga: New Moon*, Summit Entertainment, 2009

Scene: Mr. Berty notices that Edward (Robert Pattinson) and Bella (Kristen Stewart) are talking while the class watches a DVD of *Romeo and Juliet*, so he asks Edward to repeat the last few lines. Edward surprises Mr. Berty (and the rest of the class) by reciting the lines perfectly.

Inside Scoop: Stephenie Meyer drew inspiration for *New Moon* from Shakespeare's *Romeo and Juliet*.

Vocabulary in the Hint: *Iambic* means *using one unstressed syllable followed by one stressed syllable*. *Pentameter* refers to *a line of poetry with five groups*, since *penta-* means *five* and *meter* refers, in this case, to *the rhythm of poetry or music*. So *iambic pentameter* is *a line of poetry with five pairs of unstressed and stressed syllables*. William Shakespeare almost always wrote his plays and poems in iambic pentameter.

Everlasting means *lasting forever*. The opposite of *everlasting* is *temporary*, along with its awesome synonyms *ephemeral, evanescent, fleeting, fugitive, impermanent, transient,* and *transitory*. That last synonym, *fugitive*, reminds me of the 1993 Harrison Ford movie, *The Fugitive*, in which he is running from the law, moving quickly from place to place, staying in one place only **temporarily.**

Yoke in this case means *burden*. Synonyms: bondage, bonds, chains, domination, enslavement, fetters, hegemony, oppression, servitude, shackles, subjection, subjugation, thrall, tyranny. *Yoke* can also mean *connection* or *harness*, as in the **harness** that **connects** horses to a plow or cart.

Inauspicious means *unlucky*. Synonyms: infelicitous, unfortunate, unpropitious.

Righteous means *moral*. Synonym: virtuous.

Engrossing means *absorbing* or *all-consuming*.

Group 2

Here's an excerpt from a movie. See if you can name the movie, describe the scene, and define the boldface vocabulary word. Check your answers on the following page.

H.G.: Viktor's more of a physical being. (*She laughs.*) I just mean he's not particularly **loquacious.** Mostly, he watches me study. It's a bit annoying, actually. (*short pause*) You *are* trying to figure this egg out, aren't you?

Movie: _____

Scene: _____

_____

Loquacious might mean _____

_____

Hint: Viktor Krum

Solutions

Let's see how you did. Check your answers and write the exact definition. To help you memorize the vocabulary word, reread the movie excerpt or even act out the scene with a friend.

Movie: *Harry Potter and the Goblet of Fire,* Warner Bros. Pictures, 2005

Scene: Hermione (Emma Watson) and Harry (Daniel Radcliffe) are talking about Hermione's relationship with Viktor Krum (Stanislav Ianevski) and then about Harry's hint for the second task of the Triwizard Tournament.

Inside Scoop: The rock band playing at the Yule Ball includes Jonny Greenwood and Phil Selway of Radiohead as well as Jarvis Cocker from Pulp!

Loquacious means *talkative.* It's true; Viktor Krum is not very **chatty,** though he's a mighty fine Seeker (a key position in the magical sport of Quidditch). Synonyms: effusive, expansive, garrulous, pleonastic, prolix, verbose, voluble. Antonyms: reticent, taciturn. *Loq-* means *speak,* which helps you remember high-level words such as *colloquial* (informal **speaking**), *grandiloquence* (pompous **speaking**), and *obloquy* (harsh criticism).

Group 3

Here are three excerpts from a movie. See if you can name the movie, describe the scenes, and define the boldface vocabulary words. Check your answers on the following page.

ROLLO: What's the **prognosis,** fertile Myrtle? Minus or plus?

BREN: Hon, did you get expelled?

J: No, the school would most likely contact you in the event of my expulsion.

BREN: Well, I was just asking. It seemed **plausible.**

MAC: You're looking a little **morose,** honey. What's eating you?

J: I'm just, like, losing my faith with humanity . . . I just wonder if, like, two people can ever stay together for good . . .

MAC: Well, it's not easy, that's for sure. Now, I may not have the best track record in the world, I know, but I have been with your stepmother for ten years now, and I'm proud to say that we're very happy. Look, in my opinion, the best thing you can do is find a person who loves you for exactly what you are. Good mood, bad mood, ugly, pretty, handsome, what have you, the right person is still going to think the sun shines out your a*&. That's the kind of person that's worth sticking with.

Movie: _____

Scenes: _____

_____

Prognosis might mean _____

Plausible might mean _____

Morose might mean _____

Hint: "Yo, yo, yiggity-yo"

Solutions

Let's see how you did. Check your answers and write the exact definitions. To help you memorize the vocabulary words, reread the movie excerpts or even act out the scenes with a friend.

Movie: *Juno,* Fox Searchlight Pictures, 2007

Scenes: In the first excerpt, Juno comes out of the store bathroom with her pregnancy test and the clerk asks the prognosis. In the second excerpt, she tells her parents that she's pregnant, and in the third excerpt, she asks her dad about love.

Prognosis means *forecast* or *prediction*.

Plausible means *reasonable, probable,* or *believable.* Synonyms: credible, feasible. Antonyms: implausible, incredible. Since *in-* means *not, incredible* means *not credible* or *unbelievable.*

Morose means *gloomy.* Synonyms: doleful, dour, glum, lugubrious, melancholic, morbid, sullen.

Group 4

Here are two excerpts from a movie. See if you can name the movie, describe the scenes, and define the boldface vocabulary words. Check your answers on the following page.

TORRANCE: I put this to the entire squad: Swear you guys didn't know . . . I feel awful. It's **depraved.**

DARCY: Big Red ran the show, man. I mean, we were just flying **ignorami** for sobbing out loud.

TORRANCE: We can't go to Regionals with a stolen routine. It's too risky.

WHITNEY: Changing the routine now would be total murder-suicide.

COURTNEY: Seriously. Let's not put the "duh" in "dumb."

DARCY: (*at the cheerleading competition*) Remember, they give extra points for **alacrity** and **effulgence.**

KASEY: (*confused*) Did we bring those?

Movie: _____

Scenes: _____

_____

Depraved might mean _____

Ignorami might mean _____

Alacrity might mean _____

Effulgence might mean _____

Hint: "Spirit fingers!"

Solutions

Let's see how you did. Check your answers and write the exact definitions. To help you memorize the vocabulary words, reread the movie excerpts or even act out the scenes with a friend.

Movie: *Bring It On,* Universal Studios, 2000

Scenes: In the first excerpt, Torrance (Kirsten Dunst), the new cheerleading captain, tells the team that their previous team captain had stolen all their prize-winning cheers from another team. In the second excerpt, Darcy and Kasey are chatting before their cheerleading performance at Regionals.

Inside Scoop: In the film, Torrance's team is from the fictional town of Rancho Carne, which translates from Spanish as "Meat Ranch"! And here's one more fun fact: Lindsay Sloane plays Tor's totally obnoxious predecessor as team captain, whom they call Big Red. Well, ten years later she's still super obnoxious as Marnie, Kirk's ex-girlfriend, in *She's Out of My League!*

Depraved means *corrupt* or *wicked*. Synonyms: baleful, execrable, impious, iniquitous, malevolent, nefarious, pernicious, reprehensible, villainous.

Ignorami is not a commonly used word, but Darcy is trying to sound smart by making the word *ignoramus* (an ignorant person) plural. *Ignoramus* translates directly from Latin as "we do not know"; its more usual plural is *ignoramuses*. Darcy has a terrific vocabulary and is the one who uses *alacrity* and *effulgence* as well as a few other high-level words that you can look for later in this book.

Alacrity means *eagerness*. Synonyms: ardor, avidity, dispatch, fervor, keenness.

Effulgence means *brightness, radiance,* or *showing energy and joy.* The team's "spirit fingers" (this refers to when the team wiggles their fingers in the overly dramatic routine that Sparky Polastri teaches them) are **bright, radiant,** and **energetic.**

Group 5

Here's an excerpt from a movie. See if you can name the movie, describe the scene, and define the boldface vocabulary word. Check your answers on the following page.

B.J.: You once said that you liked me just as I am, and I just wanted to say *likewise*. I mean there are stupid things your mum buys you, tonight's another classic. You're **haughty,** and you always say the wrong thing in *every* situation, and I seriously believe that you should rethink the length of your sideburns. But, you're a nice man, and I like you. If you wanted to pop by some time that might be nice . . . more than nice.

Movie: _____

Scene: _____

_____

Haughty might mean _____

_____

Hint: "I decided to take control of my life and start a diary . . . "

Solutions

Let's see how you did. Check your answers and write the exact definition. To help you memorize the vocabulary word, reread the movie excerpt or even act out the scene with a friend.

Movie: *Bridget Jones's Diary,* Miramax Films, 2001

Scene: Bridget (Renée Zellweger) tells Mark Darcy (Colin Firth) how she feels about him.

Inside Scoop: Renée Zellweger took on an English accent and gained twenty-five pounds to play the role of Bridget Jones.

Haughty means *arrogant*. Synonyms: bombastic, pompous, supercilious. These are great test-prep words; *bombastic* and *supercilious* showed up on an SAT that I was reviewing just the other day. You should definitely say or write the word *haughty* and its synonyms five times—this is a great way to help you memorize a bunch of new words all at one time.

Group 6

Here's an excerpt from a movie. See if you can name the movie, describe the scene, and define the boldface vocabulary words. Check your answers on the following page.

JACK: I have every faith in your **reconciliatory** navigational skills, Master Gibbs . . . We have a need to travel upriver.

GIBBS: By need, do you mean a **trifling** need, **fleeting,** as in, say, a passing fancy?

JACK: No, a **resolute** and **unyielding** need.

WILL: . . . We *need* to . . . make sail for Port Royale with all **haste.**

JACK: William, I shall trade you the compass if you will help me to find this. (*shows a drawing of a key*)

WILL: You want me to find this?

JACK: No, *you* want you to find this. Because the finding of this finds you **incapacitorially** finding and or locating, in your discovering, the detecting a way to save your dolly belle . . .

Movie: _____

Scene: _____

Reconciliatory might mean _____

Trifling might mean _____

Fleeting might mean _____

Resolute might mean _____

Unyielding might mean _____

Haste might mean _____

Incapacitorially might mean _____

Hint: "Savvy?"

Solutions

Let's see how you did. Check your answers and write the exact definitions. To help you memorize the vocabulary words, reread the movie excerpt or even act out the scene with a friend.

Movie: *Pirates of the Caribbean: Dead Man's Chest,* Walt Disney Pictures, 2006

Scene: Will Turner's (Orlando Bloom) fiancée, Elizabeth (Keira Knightley), has been arrested by Lord Beckett (Tom Hollander) for helping Captain Jack Sparrow (Johnny Depp) to escape execution. Lord Becket has offered to release and pardon Elizabeth if Will can obtain Jack's compass. The compass takes its wielder wherever she or he most truly wants to go.

Vocabulary in the Hint: *Savvy* means *understand.* Captain Jack Sparrow is using this word as a verb: "Savvy?" meaning "Do you understand?" The word can also be used as a noun to mean *understanding* or *knowledge,* especially *practical, rather than theoretical, knowledge,* such as in business or politics.

Reconciliatory means *settling, resolving,* or *making consistent.*

Trifling means *unimportant.* Synonyms: exiguous, incidental, negligible, nominal, nugatory, pettifogging, petty, trivial.

Fleeting means *disappearing quickly,* like "a passing fancy." Synonyms: ephemeral, evanescent, fugitive, impermanent, transient, transitory.

Resolute means *determined.* Synonyms: staunch, steadfast, unswerving.

Unyielding means *stubborn, unbending,* or *determined.* Synonyms: dogged, intractable, intransigent, obdurate, obstinate, pertinacious, tenacious.

Haste means *speed.* A very high-level synonym for *haste* is *expedition,* so Will could have said, "What we need to do is make sail for Port Royale with all **expedition.**" *Expedition,* can also mean *a journey*.

Incapacitorially means . . . well . . . actually, it's not a word in English; Captain Jack made it up.

Group 7

Here's an excerpt from a movie. See if you can name the movie, describe the scene, and define the boldface vocabulary words. Check your answers on the following page.

SECRETARY CLEARY: John, you seem like an **astute** man. Maybe you can help explain something to me. See that young man out there on the dock? (*points to a young man in a tuxedo gloomily picking petals off a rose*) That's my son, Todd. Twenty-two years old, the whole world in front of him, every advantage in life . . . What's he got to be so **morose** about?

JOHN: Maybe he hasn't found something to believe in . . . Maybe he's just trying to find his own way, his own path.

Movie: _____

Scene: _____

_____

Astute might mean _____

_____

Morose might mean _____

_____

Hint #1: This excerpt takes place at a wedding, and John is not *really* supposed to be there.
Hint #2: Rule #96: **Etiquette** isn't old-fashioned. It's sexy.

Solutions

Let's see how you did. Check your answers and write the exact definitions. To help you memorize the vocabulary words, reread the movie excerpt or even act out the scene with a friend.

Movie: *Wedding Crashers* (Uncorked Edition), New Line Cinema, 2005

Scene: John (Owen Wilson) and Senator Cleary (Christopher Walken) are standing on a dock chatting. I find this movie oddly inspiring. I don't aspire to crash weddings, but I appreciate the friendship of John and Jeremy (Vince Vaughn) and the transformation and insight of John's character as he falls in love with Claire (Rachel McAdams) and goes from insensitive, unethical wedding crasher to sensitive, honest romantic.

Inside Scoop: Did you recognize Rachel McAdams as queen bee Regina George from *Mean Girls?*

Vocabulary in the Hint: *Etiquette* means *proper or polite behavior.* Synonyms: decorum, propriety, protocol.

Astute means *intelligent and insightful.* Synonyms: canny, incisive, judicious, keen, perspicacious, sagacious, savvy, shrewd, wise. The synonym *keen* can also mean *eager.*

Morose means *gloomy.* You first learned this word on the *Juno* page (Group 3), when Juno's dad said, "You're looking a little **morose,** honey. What's eating you?" Synonyms: doleful, dour, glum, lugubrious, melancholic, morbid, sullen.

Group 8

Here are three excerpts from a movie. See if you can name the movie, describe the scenes, and define the boldface vocabulary words. Check your answers on the following page.

Lena: (*points to a dress*) How about this one?

Tibby: It's great if you want to go to Greece looking like Laverne De Fazio.

Lena: Who?

Tibby: '70s TV **icon.** Am I the only one who's not culturally deprived around here?

———————

Bridget: Oh please, you're the one who wanted to stay here all summer and **angst** it out making your documentary . . .

Tibby: You know, I think I'm going to start my own **genre,** call it the "suckumentary."

———————

Lena: We need rules. Every sisterhood has rules.

Carmen: Thank you. A **manifesto.** Good point. I love it. OK, rule number one . . .

Movie: _____

Scenes: _____

Icon might mean _____

Angst might mean _____

Genre might mean _____

Manifesto might mean _____

Hint: "We're the sisters of these *pantalones*."

Solutions

Let's see how you did. Check your answers and write the exact definitions. To help you memorize the vocabulary words, reread the movie excerpts or even act out the scenes with a friend.

Movie: *The Sisterhood of the Traveling Pants,* Warner Bros., 2005

Scenes: In the first and second excerpts, the girls are chatting while browsing in a vintage clothing store where they find the mighty pants of the movie title. (The pants mysteriously fit all four girls even though the girls are different heights and sizes.) In the third excerpt, they are creating the rules of the Sisterhood.

Inside Scoop: This was Blake Lively's (Bridget) breakout role. She filmed the movie between her junior and senior years of high school. Her father, Ernie Lively, who is also an actor, actually plays her father in the movie! After this film, she went on to star as Serena van der Woodsen in *Gossip Girl.*

Icon means *symbol,* just like the small pictures (icons) on your computer screen are **symbols** of applications and files. Tibby (Amber Tamblyn) means that Laverne (from the TV show *Laverne and Shirley*) is a symbol of 1970s TV. It's true, she's right up there with the Fonz and the *Brady Bunch.* Synonym: paragon. The word *icon* helps you remember the high-level standardized test word *iconoclast* (one who attacks established beliefs— literally one who breaks **icons**).

Angst in this case is a verb that means *struggle* or *face discomfort.* Usually *angst* is used as a noun that means *anxiety* or *uneasiness.* Synonyms: disquietude, trepidation.

Genre means *artistic category,* like romantic comedies or bromances.

Manifesto means *declaration of policy.* Synonyms: credo, creed, mission statement, platform.

Here's an excerpt from a movie. See if you can name the movie, describe the scene, and define the boldface vocabulary word. Check your answers on the following page.

TOULA PORTOKALOS: When I was growing up, I knew I was different. The other girls were blonde and delicate, and I was a **swarthy** six-year-old with sideburns.

Movie: _____

Scene: _____

_____

Swarthy might mean _____

_____

Hint: "Give me a word, any word, and I show you how the root of that word is Greek. How about *arachnophobia*? *Arachna*, that come from the Greek word for *spider*. And *phobia* mean *fear*. So, *fear of spider*, there you go."

Solutions

Let's see how you did. Check your answers and write the exact definition. To help you memorize the vocabulary word, reread the movie excerpt or even act out the scene with a friend.

Movie: *My Big Fat Greek Wedding,* IFC Films, 2002

Scene: Early in the movie, Toula (Nia Vardalos) narrates a flashback of herself at age six.

Inside Scoop: Ian is played by John Corbett, who also plays Carrie's ex, Aidan Shaw, in *Sex and the City.*

Vocabulary in the Hint: Toula's father, Gus (Michael Constantine), lays out a beautiful vocabulary lesson for you here. *Phobia* does mean *fear.* That helps you with words like *aerophobia* (*aero* means *air,* so *fear of flying*), *emetophobia* (*emet-* is like *emit,* which means *discharge,* or basically *puke,* so *fear of vomiting*), and *necrophobia* (*necro-* means *death,* so *fear of death*). *Phobia* is not the only Greek word that you can learn from Gus in this film. For example, he uses the word *xenos* to refer to all non-Greeks, such as Toula's boyfriend, Ian. In Greek, *xeno* means *foreigner.* That helps you remember high-level vocabulary words such as *xenophobic* (afraid of foreigners) and *xenophile* (one who loves or is interested in foreign people, ideas, and objects).

Swarthy means *dark-skinned.* The word *swarthy* reminds me of a hilarious scene from *The Proposal.* Remember the absurd and somewhat disturbing lap dance that the exotic dancer Ramone (Oscar Nuñez from *The Office*) gave Sandra Bullock's character? After that dance, Ramone was quite taken with her, and at the end of the movie he tells the immigration agent, "In my mind I see her with someone, perhaps, more **swarthy**—darker," meaning himself.

Group 10

Here's an excerpt from a movie. See if you can name the movie, describe the scene, and define the boldface vocabulary words. Check your answers on the following page.

BRIONY TALLIS (AGE 13): The princess was well aware of his **remorseless** wickedness. But that made it no easier to overcome the **voluminous** love she felt in her heart for Sir Romulus. The princess knew instinctively that the one with red hair was not to be trusted. As his young **ward** dived again and again into the depths of the lake in search of the enchanted **chalice,** Sir Romulus twirled his luxuriant mustache. Sir Romulus rode with his two companions, northwards, drawing ever closer to an **effulgent** sea. So heroic in manner, he appeared so **valiant** in word. And no one could ever guess at the darkness lurking in the black heart of Sir Romulus Turnbull. He was the most dangerous man in the world.

Movie: _____

Scene: _____

_____

Remorseless might mean _____

Voluminous might mean _____

Ward might mean _____

Chalice might mean _____

Effulgent might mean _____

Valiant might mean _____

Hint: A synonym for this film's title is *expiation.*

Solutions

Let's see how you did. Check your answers and write the exact definitions. To help you memorize the vocabulary words, reread the movie excerpt or even act out the scene with a friend.

Movie: *Atonement,* Focus Features, 2007

Scene: Briony Tallis (Saoirse Ronan), at age thirteen, writes *fanciful* (imaginative) stories and plays. The stories reflect her own thoughts, experiences, and struggles, such as her crush on Robbie (James McAvoy), son of the Tallis' housekeeper.

Vocabulary in the Hint: *Expiation* means *atonement* (the act of making up for a sin or bad deed). In the film, at age thirteen, Briony falsely accuses Robbie of rape, and as a result of her false accusation, Robbie is sent to jail. Later in life, Briony tries to **make up for** this irresponsible action.

Remorseless means *without regret.* Synonyms: callous, merciless, pitiless, ruthless.

Voluminous means *plentiful—with lots of volume.* Synonyms: abundant, bounteous, capacious, commodious, prodigious, profuse, prolific.

Ward means *person looked after or protected by another* and comes from the old French word for *guard,* which is why guards are sometimes called *wardens.*

Chalice means *cup* or *goblet,* like the chalice referred to as the Holy Grail in *Indiana Jones and the Last Crusade* or *The Da Vinci Code.*

Effulgent means *radiant.* It can mean **radiating** happiness or **radiating** brightness, like the sunshine on a clear lake. Synonym: ebullient. Remember this word from *Bring It On* in Group 4? Darcy says, " . . . they give extra points for **alacrity** and **effulgence**," meaning **eagerness** and **radiant joy and energy.**

Valiant means *brave.* Synonyms: audacious, dauntless, doughty, gallant, indomitable, intrepid, lionhearted, valorous. Antonym: cowardly.

Quiz 1

I. Let's review some of the words that you've seen in Groups 1–10. Match each of the following words to the correct definition or synonym on the right. If you need help, refer back to the movie excerpts and definitions. Then check the solutions on page 237.

1. Inauspicious	A. Verbose
2. Loquacious	B. Iniquitous
3. Morose	C. Radiance
4. Depraved	D. Supercilious
5. Alacrity	E. Unpropitious
6. Effulgence	F. Lugubrious
7. Haughty	G. Judicious
8. Fleeting	H. Ardor
9. Trifling	I. Steadfast
10. Resolute	J. Nugatory
11. Haste	K. One who attacks cherished beliefs
12. Astute	
13. Iconoclast	L. Profuse
14. Expiation	M. Evanescent
15. Voluminous	N. Expedition
	O. Atonement

II. Let's review several of the word parts that you've seen in Groups 1–10. Match each of the following word parts to the correct definition or synonym on the right. Then check the solutions on page 237.

16. Loq- (as in *loquacious*)	A. Not
17. In- (as in *incredible*)	B. Death
18. Icon- (as in *iconoclast*)	C. Speak
19. Aero- (as in *aerophobia*)	D. Foreigner
20. Necro- (as in *necrophobia*)	E. Air
21. Xeno- (as in *xenophobic*)	F. Symbol

III. Match each group of synonyms to its general meaning. Then check the solutions on page 237.

22. Effusive
    Expansive
    Loquacious
    Prolix
    Verbose
    Voluble

A. Gloomy

23. Doleful
    Dour
    Lugubrious
    Melancholic
    Morose
    Sullen

B. Arrogant

24. Baleful
    Depraved
    Execrable
    Impious
    Iniquitous
    Malevolent
    Nefarious
    Pernicious

C. Disappearing quickly

25. Bombastic
    Haughty
    Pompous
    Supercilious

D. Talkative

26. Ephemeral
    Evanescent
    Fleeting
    Fugitive
    Transient

E. Wicked

Group 11

Here are four excerpts from a movie. See if you can name the movie, describe the scenes, and define the boldface vocabulary words. Check your answers on the following pages.

ELIZABETH: Are you too proud, Mr. Darcy? And would you consider pride a fault or a **virtue**?

MR. DARCY: That I couldn't say.

ELIZABETH: Because we're doing our best to find a fault in you.

MR. DARCY: Maybe it's that I find it hard to forgive the **follies** and **vices** of others or their offenses against me. My good opinion once lost, is lost forever.

ELIZABETH: Did I just agree to dance with Mr. Darcy?

CHARLOTTE: I dare say you will find him very **amiable**, Lizzy.

ELIZABETH: It would be most inconvenient since I have sworn to **loathe** him for all eternity. (*Elizabeth and Charlotte giggle.*)

MR. DARCY: Do you talk as a rule while dancing?

ELIZABETH: No, I prefer to be unsociable and **taciturn**.

MR. DARCY: I love you most **ardently**. Please do me the honor of accepting my hand.

Movie: _____

Scenes: _____

_____

Hint: This movie is based on a book that you might have read in English class.

Group 11 (continued)

Virtue might mean _____

_____

Follies might mean _____

_____

Vices might mean _____

_____

Amiable might mean _____

_____

Loathe might mean _____

_____

Taciturn might mean _____

_____

Ardently might mean _____

_____

Solutions

Let's see how you did. Check your answers and write the exact definitions. To help you memorize the vocabulary words, reread the movie excerpts or even act out the scenes with a friend.

Movie: *Pride & Prejudice,* Focus Features, 2005

Scenes: This movie takes place in nineteenth-century England. In the first excerpt, Elizabeth (Keira Knightley) is visiting her sister at Mr. Bingley's country estate and strikes up a conversation with Bingley's friend, Mr. Darcy (Matthew Macfadyen). In the second excerpt, Elizabeth and her best friend, Charlotte, are discussing Mr. Darcy at a ball. In the third, Elizabeth is dancing with Darcy, and in the fourth, Darcy proclaims his love for her. This is a must-see movie. It's romantic, witty, and touching. It's *Twilight* without the vampires. And it's absolutely full of excellent vocabulary! I could write a vocabulary book just on this movie. Watch it five times and your vocabulary will improve, guaranteed!

Inside Scoop: The actors who play lovebirds Mr. Bingley (Simon Woods) and Jane Bennet (Rosamund Pike) had actually dated two years earlier while in college at Oxford.

Virtue means *good quality.* The opposite of *virtue* is *vice,* a bad quality. Synonyms: rectitude, righteousness.

Follies means *foolishness.* Synonyms: imprudence, indiscretion, injudiciousness, rashness, recklessness.

Vices means *immoral behaviors.* Synonyms: corruption, debauchery, decadence, degeneracy, depravity, dissipation, dissolution, iniquity, lechery, perversion, transgression, trespass, turpitude, villainy.

Amiable means *friendly and pleasant* and comes from the Latin word *amicus,* which means *friend,* like *amigo* in Spanish, or *ami* in French. Synonyms: affable, amicable, convivial, cordial, genial, gregarious, simpatico.

Loathe means *hate.* Synonyms: abhor, condemn, despise, detest, disdain, execrate, scorn.

Taciturn means *not talkative.* Synonyms: introverted, reserved, reticent.

Ardently means *eagerly* or *passionately.* Synonyms: avidly, fervently, keenly, zealously.

Group 12

Here are two excerpts from a movie. See if you can name the movie, describe the scenes, and define the boldface vocabulary words. Check your answers on the following page.

CAL: We're running out of time. (*motions toward a crew member who is admitting passengers onto lifeboats*) This strutting **martinet** isn't letting any men on at all.

LOVEJOY: There's one on the other side letting men on.

CAL: Well then, that's our play.

ROSE (AGE 100): Afterward, the 700 people in the boats had nothing to do but wait. Wait to die, wait to live, wait for an **absolution** that would never come.

Movie: _____

Scenes: _____

_____

Martinet might mean _____

_____

Absolution might mean _____

_____

Hint: "Iceberg, right ahead!"

Solutions

Let's see how you did. Check your answers and write the exact definitions. To help you memorize the vocabulary words, reread the movie excerpts or even act out the scenes with a friend.

Movie: *Titanic,* Paramount Pictures, 1997

Scenes: In the first excerpt, the ship (the *Titanic*) is going down after hitting an iceberg. There are not enough lifeboats, so the crew is putting women and children into the lifeboats first. In the second excerpt, 100-year-old Rose finishes telling her story of surviving the sinking of the *Titanic.*

Inside Scoop: *Titanic* was the highest-grossing film of all time for twelve years running, until *Avatar* took the title in 2009. Amazingly, James Cameron made both films!

Vocabulary in the Title: *Titanic,* of course, refers to the name of the famous ship that is going down, but it also means *very large, strong, and powerful.* That's why Mr. Ismay, the director of the company that owns the *Titanic,* named the ship *Titanic,* to convey that it was the newest, **largest,** and **most powerful** ship on the seas. In fact, there is a hilarious bit of dialogue in which Mr. Ismay states, "I wanted to convey sheer **size.** And size means stability, luxury, and above all **strength,**" to which Rose sasses, "Do you know of Dr. Freud, Mr. Ismay? His ideas about the male preoccupation with size might be of particular interest to you." Synonyms: colossal, inordinate, mammoth, monumental, prodigious.

Martinet means *strict disciplinarian.* Synonyms: doctrinaire, dogmatist, pedant, stickler.

Absolution means *forgiveness.* Synonyms: acquittal, clemency, dispensation, exculpation, exoneration, indulgence, shrift. Antonym: condemnation.

Group 13

Here's an excerpt from a movie. See if you can name the movie, describe the scene, and define the boldface vocabulary words. Check your answers on the following page.

BURKE: I happen to know a thing or two about people. You get approached a lot; probably have since the day you strapped on your first training bra. But you're smart, and you're creative, and you're caring and deep. But, how come the guys only see the package it comes in? Sure, you're flattered. But ultimately, ultimately it's tiresome because it has nothing to do with you. You were born that way. You can't take credit for it. Your insides though, that's yours. That's what you want someone to truly see. Even a stranger. **Ergo,** you fake a handicap rather than **deign** to have a conversation with a fellow human being. You prefer sign language? Fine. (*gives her "the finger"*)

Movie: _____

Scene: _____

_____

Ergo might mean _____

_____

Deign might mean _____

_____

Hint: In this film, Eloise has a quirky habit of writing unusual words behind paintings in public places. Burke finds three: *quidnunc, poppysmic,* and *sesquipedalianist.*

Solutions

Let's see how you did. Check your answers and write the exact definitions. To help you memorize the vocabulary words, reread the movie excerpt or even act out the scene with a friend.

Movie: *Love Happens,* Universal Pictures, 2009

Scene: Early in the movie, Burke (Aaron Eckhart) tries to ask out Eloise (Jennifer Aniston), a girl he just met, but she blows him off using sign language. Later he overhears her having a spoken conversation so he gets angry and delivers this monologue.

Vocabulary in the Hint: *Quidnunc* means *a gossipy person, poppysmic* refers to *the sound of one's lips smacking,* and *sesquipedalianist* means *a person who uses very long words.* Luckily, you won't see these three words on the SAT, but **sesquipedalianist** comes from *sesquipedalian,* which means *long-winded* and is a great review of a word you just learned. Do you remember what terrific standardized test synonyms you learned for *long-winded?* Hint: "Viktor's more of a physical being. (*She laughs.*) I just mean he's not particularly --------." Answer: In *Harry Potter and the Goblet of Fire* (Group 2), Hermione said that Viktor Krum was not *loquacious* (talkative). Synonyms for *loquacious:* effusive, expansive, garrulous, pleonastic, prolix, verbose, voluble.

Ergo means *therefore.* Synonyms: consequently, hence, whence.

Deign resembles the first half of *dignity* and means *do something beneath one's dignity.* That's a great way to remember this word, or you could just memorize Burke's angry monologue. Synonyms: condescend, demean oneself, vouchsafe.

Group 14

Here's an excerpt from a movie. See if you can name the movie, describe the scene, and define the boldface vocabulary words. Check your answers on the following page.

BOB: Just because you have no **semblance** of a life outside of this office, you think that you can treat all of us like your own personal slaves. You know what? I feel sorry for you because do you know what you're going to have on your deathbed? Nothing and no one.

MARGARET: Listen carefully, Bob. I didn't fire you because I feel threatened. No, I fired you because you're lazy, **entitled,** incompetent, and you spend more time cheating on your wife than you do in your office. And if you say another word, Andrew here is going to have you thrown out . . . Another word, and you're going out of here with an armed escort. Andrew will film it with his little camera phone and put it on that Internet site.

Movie: _____

Scene: _____

Semblance might mean _____

_____

Entitled might mean _____

_____

Hint: "Three days ago, I **loathed** you. I used to dream about you getting hit by a cab or poisoned . . . Then we had our little adventure up in Alaska and things started to change. Things changed when we kissed, and when you told me about your tattoo, even when you checked me out when we were naked . . . But I didn't realize any of this, until I was standing alone, in a barn, wifeless. Now, you could imagine my disappointment when it suddenly dawned on me that the woman I love is about to be kicked out of the country. So, Margaret, marry me, because I'd like to date you."

Solutions

Let's see how you did. Check your answers and write the exact definitions. To help you memorize the vocabulary words, reread the movie excerpt or even act out the scene with a friend.

Movie: *The Proposal,* Touchstone Pictures, 2009

Scene: Margaret Tate (Sandra Bullock) is editor in chief at Ruick & Hunt Publishing. She fires Bob, who is an editor at the firm, and he yells at her with these lines. She plays it cool in her response, but later admits to Andrew (Ryan Reynolds) that after Bob's *diatribe* (angry, attacking speech) she cried in the bathroom.

Inside Scoop: Sandra Bullock's hilarious hip-hop dance in the woods with Gammy is to Lil' Jon's "Get Low."

Vocabulary in the Hint: *Loathed* means *hated*. Synonyms for *loathe:* abhor, condemn, despise, detest, disdain, execrate, scorn. Antonym: love.

Semblance means *appearance* or *similarity*. In French, *sembler* means *to appear*—watch for similarities to words in other languages that can give you a hint to a word's meaning. Synonym: resemblance.

Entitled means *having a right.* When used as an insult, as Sandra Bullock's character uses it in the excerpt, it means *believing one has a right to more than one does.* Margaret is saying that Bob **believes that he has a right** to be an editor, yet he does not work hard or perform competently.

Group 15

Here's an excerpt from a movie. See if you can name the movie, describe the scene, and define the boldface vocabulary words. Check your answers on the following page.

Ms. Darbus: Perhaps the most **heinous** example of cell phone abuse is ringing in the theater. What **temerity!** The theater is a temple of art. A precious **cornucopia** of creative energy . . .

Coach Bolton: What the heck are those two doing in a tree?

Ms. Darbus: It's called crime and punishment, Bolton. Besides, **proximity** to the arts is cleansing for the soul.

Movie: _____

Scene: _____

_____

Heinous might mean _____

_____

Temerity might mean _____

_____

Cornucopia might mean _____

_____

Proximity might mean _____

_____

Hint: This 2006 movie has been called a modern retelling of Shakespeare's *Romeo and Juliet*—a boy and girl from different social circles find romance on a New Year's Eve karaoke stage.

Solutions

Let's see how you did. Check your answers and write the exact definitions. To help you memorize the vocabulary words, reread the movie excerpt or even act out the scene with a friend.

Movie: *High School Musical,* Disney Channel, 2006

Scene: In this scene, two of East High School's star basketball players, Troy (Zac Efron) and Chad (Corbin Blue), are serving detention with Ms. Darbus because their cell phones rang during her class. Their detention involves painting sets for the school's musical, and their coach, Coach Bolton, who is also Troy's father, is furious when he finds out that his players are missing practice to be in Ms. Darbus' detention.

Heinous means *wicked* or *repulsive.* Synonyms: abhorrent, abominable, atrocious, contemptible, despicable, detestable, egregious, execrable, horrific, iniquitous, loathsome, monstrous, odious, reprehensible, unspeakable, villainous. I think the very *grandiloquent* (pompously speaking) Ms. Darbus would have used all of these synonyms if there had been time.

Temerity means *bold rudeness.* Synonyms: audacity, chutzpah, effrontery, gall, impertinence, impudence, nerve, presumption.

Cornucopia means *abundance.* You may have seen this word in Suzanne Collins' novel *The Hunger Games.* The cornucopia is the giant golden horn in the center of the tributes when the "games" begin. The cornucopia holds an **abundance** of supplies and gear that the tributes need. Synonyms: bounty, profusion.

Proximity means *nearness.* Synonym: propinquity.

Group 16

Here are three excerpts from a movie. See if you can name the movie, describe the scenes, and define the boldface vocabulary words. Check your answers on the following page.

CHER: I felt **impotent** and out of control, which I really hate. I needed to find **sanctuary** in a place where I could gather my thoughts and regain my strength. (*goes to the mall*)

_____

CHER: Will you look at that body language? Legs crossed towards each other; that's an **unequivocal** sex invite.

_____

CHER: That's another thing, Tai. We've got to work on your accent and vocabulary. See, *sporadic* means *once in a while*. Try and use it in a sentence today.

Movie: _____

Scenes: _____

Impotent might mean _____

Sanctuary might mean _____

Unequivocal might mean _____

Sporadic might mean _____

Hint: **DIONNE:** "Rough winds do shake the darling buds of May, but thy eternal summer shall not fade." Phat! Did you write that?

CHER: Duh, it's like a famous quote.

DIONNE: From where?

CHER: CliffsNotes.

Solutions

Let's see how you did. Check your answers and write the exact definitions. To help you memorize the vocabulary words, reread the movie excerpts or even act out the scenes with a friend.

Movie: *Clueless,* Paramount Pictures, 1995

Scenes: Before the first excerpt, Cher (Alicia Silverstone) had tried and failed to argue for a higher grade in her high school debate class. She feels defeated and seeks refuge and comfort at the mall. She decides that her teacher, Mr. Hall, is difficult because he's lonely, so she plans to set him up with her world history teacher, Miss Geist. In the second excerpt, she admires the success of her matchmaking while watching the two teachers sitting on a bench at school. In the third excerpt, she has taken on a new project, to turn a new student, Tai Frasier (Brittany Murphy), into a hip coolster.

Inside Scoop: I was shocked by all of the amazing vocabulary words in *Clueless,* but then recalled that it is a modern retelling of Jane Austin's novel *Emma.* Jane knows her vocab, and her matchmaking.

Literature in the Hint: "Rough winds do shake the darling buds of May, but thy eternal summer shall not fade" is from one of Shakespeare's most famous poems, *Sonnet 18,* which begins, "Shall I compare thee to a summer's day?"

Impotent means *powerless. Im-* means *not,* and *potent* means *powerful,* as in *omnipotent* (all powerful), so *impotent* means *not powerful—powerless.* Synonyms: feeble, impuissant.

Sanctuary means *a place or feeling of safety and comfort.* Synonyms: haven, refuge.

Unequivocal means *definite.* Synonyms: categorical, incontrovertible, indubitable, unconditional, unqualified. Remember to say or write the word *unequivocal* and its synonyms five times. Memorizing this list is a great way to memorize a bunch of high-level standardized-test vocabulary words all at one time.

Sporadic means *irregularly occurring* or as Cher says, "Once in a while." Synonyms: desultory, erratic, intermittent.

Here's an excerpt from a movie. See if you can name the movie, describe the scene, and define the boldface vocabulary words. Check your answers on the following page.

NARRATOR: Southern summers are **indifferent** to the trials of young love. Armed with warnings and doubts, Noah and Allie gave a remarkably convincing portrayal of a boy and a girl traveling down a very long road with no regard for the **consequences.**

Movie: _____

Scene: _____

_____

Indifferent might mean _____

_____

Consequences might mean _____

_____

Hint: "It was an **improbable** romance: He was a country boy, she was from the city; she had the world at her feet, while he didn't have two dimes to rub together."

Solutions

Let's see how you did. Check your answers and write the exact definitions. To help you memorize the vocabulary words, reread the movie excerpt or even act out the scene with a friend.

Movie: *The Notebook,* New Line Cinema, 2004

Scene: Duke (James Garner) is narrating the story of when Noah (Ryan Gosling) and Allie (Rachel McAdams) first fell in love.

Inside Scoop: Ryan Gosling is now famous for *The Notebook, Half Nelson,* and *Lars and the Real Girl,* but he actually got his start as a cast member on the Disney Channel's *The All-New Mickey Mouse Club,* where he was a cast member along with Britney Spears, Christina Aguilera, Justin Timberlake, J.C. Chasez, and Keri Russell!

Vocabulary in the Hint: *Improbable* means *unlikely.* Synonyms: absurd, dubious, fanciful, inconceivable.

Indifferent means *uninterested* or *unconcerned.* This is an interesting word to break apart. *In-* means *not,* so *indifferent* means *not noticing differences—* being **uninterested** or **unconcerned.** Synonyms: apathetic, cavalier, dismissive, dispassionate, impassive, insouciant, nonchalant, perfunctory. All of these words imply *not being interested* or *not caring.*

Consequences means *results,* usually *negative results.* An awesome high-level synonym for *consequences* is *ramifications.* Use that word correctly in your essay, and you're sure to gain a point. Synonyms: aftermath, ramifications, repercussions.

Group 18

Here's an excerpt from a movie. See if you can name the movie, describe the scene, and define the boldface vocabulary word. Check your answers on the following page.

STORE CLERK: (*switching price tags on a dress*) There's nothing I love more than a dumb blonde with daddy's plastic . . . (*walking over with the dress*) Did you see this one? We just got it in yesterday.

ELLE: Oh, is this low-**viscosity** rayon?

STORE CLERK: Ahh, yes. Of course.

ELLE: With a half-loop top stitching on the hem?

STORE CLERK: Absolutely, it's one of a kind.

ELLE: It's impossible to use a half-loop top stitching on low-viscosity rayon; it would snag the fabric. And you didn't just get it in—I saw it in the June *Vogue* a year ago. So, if you're trying to sell it to me for full price, you've picked the wrong girl.

Movie: _____

Scene: _____

_____

Viscosity might mean _____

_____

Hint: Reese Witherspoon

Solutions

Let's see how you did. Check your answers and write the exact definition. To help you memorize the vocabulary word, reread the movie excerpt or even act out the scene with a friend.

Movie: *Legally Blonde,* Metro-Goldwyn-Mayer, 2001

Scene: Elle (Reese Witherspoon) thinks her boyfriend is going to propose at dinner and is shopping for a new dress to wear to the date. The store clerk sees Elle and plans to overcharge her for a dress, but Elle shows her! Elle's brilliant logic in this scene *foreshadows* (is a sign of) her future ability as a lawyer.

Inside Scoop: Reese Witherspoon's character shows up with more than twenty different hairstyles in the film. She also wears some pretty wild outfits, all of which her contract specifically stipulated she keep after filming!

Viscosity means *gooeyness*. Of course the dress is not **gooey,** but when rayon fabric is manufactured, a *viscous* (gooey) substance is hardened into fibers. So, **low-viscosity rayon** would have less viscosity than ordinary rayon, probably during the liquid stage of the manufacturing process. *Viscosity,* along with the related word *viscous* (gooey), appears quite often on standardized tests. Thanks to Elle's extensive fashion knowledge, you'll know these words and get the questions correct! Synonyms for *viscous*: gelatinous, glutinous, mucilaginous, mucoid, mucous, treacly, viscid, viscoelastic.

Here are two excerpts from a movie. See if you can name the movie, describe the scenes, and define the boldface vocabulary words. Check your answers on the following pages.

Ms. Perky: (*writing at her computer*) **Undulating** with desire, Adrienne removes her **crimson** cape . . . (*yells to her secretary*) Judith, what's another word for **engorged?**

Judith: I'll look it up.

Ms. Perky: OK . . . Swollen. **Turgid.**

Kat: (*enters Ms. Perky's office*) **Tumescent.**

Ms. Perky: Perfect. So, I hear you were terrorizing Mr. Morgan's class again.

Kat: Expressing my opinion is not a terrorist action . . .

Ms. Perky: The point is, Kat, people perceive you as somewhat . . .

Kat: Tempestuous.

Ms. Perky: "**Heinous** bitch" is the term used most often. You might want to work on that.

Joey: (*showing Bianca two photos of himself modeling*) OK, now, this is really important. OK? Which one do you like better?

Bianca: I think I like the white shirt better.

Joey: Yeah, it's more . . .

Bianca: Pensive?

Joey: Damn, I was going for *thoughtful*.

Movie: _____

Scenes: _____

Hint: One of the movie posters for this film read, "Romeo, Oh Romeo, Get Out of My Face."

Group 19 (continued)

Undulating might mean _____

_____

Crimson might mean _____

_____

Engorged might mean _____

_____

Turgid might mean _____

_____

Tumescent might mean _____

_____

Tempestuous might mean _____

_____

Heinous might mean _____

_____

Pensive might mean _____

_____

Solutions

Let's see how you did. Check your answers and write the exact definitions. To help you memorize the vocabulary words, reread the movie excerpts or even act out the scenes with a friend.

Movie: *10 Things I Hate About You,* Touchstone Pictures, 1999

Scenes: In the first excerpt, Ms. Perky (Allison Janney), the guidance counselor, is writing a scene for her porn novel when a student, Kat (Julia Stiles), arrives for a counseling session. In the second excerpt, Joey (Andrew Keegan) asks Bianca's (Larisa Oleynik) opinion of his modeling photos. Bianca and Kat are sisters, and Bianca has a crush on Joey, until she realizes how superficial he is.

Inside Scoop: This film is based on Shakespeare's *The Taming of the Shrew*. The film's title, *10 Things I Hate About You,* even sounds like *The Taming of the Shrew*—say both titles out loud and you'll hear it.

Wisdom in the Film: Thanks to Heath Ledger, who plays Patrick, for delivering the line, "Don't let anyone ever make you feel like you don't deserve what you want." Good wisdom for those in high school, or for anyone, for that matter. We miss you, Heath!

Solutions (continued)

Undulating means *moving in a flowing, wavelike motion.*

Crimson means *purplish-red.*

Engorged means *swollen.* Synonyms: distended, tumescent, tumid, turgid.

Turgid means *swollen.* Synonyms: distended, engorged, tumescent, tumid.

Tumescent means *swollen.* Synonyms: distended, engorged, tumid, turgid. *Tumescent* is also the medical term for *erect.* Interestingly, *turgid* and *tumescent* can also refer to *pompous language*—speaking or writing in a way that is self-important, pretentious, inflated, and **swollen.**

Tempestuous means *stormy* and can refer to a person who is *quick-tempered.*

Heinous means *wicked* or *hated.* Synonyms: baleful, depraved, impious, iniquitous, malevolent, nefarious, pernicious.

Pensive means *thinking deeply* and reminds me of the Pensieve in *Harry Potter and the Half-Blood Prince* that Harry and Dumbledore use to watch stored **thoughts.** Synonyms: brooding, contemplative, introspective, meditative, musing, reflective, ruminative.

Group 20

Here are two excerpts from a movie. See if you can name the movie, describe the scenes, and define the boldface vocabulary words. Check your answers on the following page.

JULIE: I forgot to tell you . . . do you know what Annabelle's doing now? Sarah told me. A blog.

ERIC: Of what?

JULIE: What do you mean of what? A blog of Annabelle. Of every thought that passes through her brain. Her stupid, **vapid, insipid** . . . I could write a blog. I have thoughts.

JULIA: (*on a TV cooking show*) I'm gonna try to flip this thing over now, which is a rather daring thing to do.

JULIE: (*watching Julia on TV*) She changed everything. Before her it was frozen food and can openers and marshmallows.

ERIC: Don't knock marshmallows.

JULIA: (*on TV*) When you flip anything, you've just got to have the courage of your **convictions**. Especially if it's a loose sort of mass. (*She flips it.*) Ohh, that didn't go very well. But you see, when I flipped it, I didn't have the courage I needed, the way I should have. But you can always put it together.

Movie: _____

Scenes: _____

_____

Vapid might mean _____

Insipid might mean _____

Convictions might mean _____

Hint: "Bon appétit!"

Solutions

Let's see how you did. Check your answers and write the exact definitions. To help you memorize the vocabulary words, reread the movie excerpts or even act out the scenes with a friend.

Movie: *Julie & Julia,* Columbia Pictures, 2009

Scenes: In the first excerpt, Julie (Amy Adams) is angry that her friend Annabelle featured her in an unflattering story in *New York* magazine. That's when she has the idea, "I could write a blog." In the second excerpt, Julie and her husband Eric (Chris Messina) are watching Julia Child on TV.

Vocabulary in the Hint: *Bon appétit* translates from French as *good appetite* and means *enjoy the meal.* Julia Child is famous for using this expression on her television show. The French word *bon* (good) helps you remember vocabulary words such as *bonhomie* (**good** nature—friendliness), *bonny* (**good** looking), and *bonanza* (**good** fortune—jackpot).

Vapid means *dull and ordinary.* Synonyms: hackneyed, insipid, jejune, lackluster, pedestrian, prosaic, trite, vacuous.

Insipid means *flavorless, dull, and uninteresting.* Synonyms: hackneyed, jejune, lackluster, pedestrian, prosaic, trite, vacuous, vapid.

Convictions means *firmly held beliefs* and comes from the word *convince;* when you have *conviction,* you are totally *convinced—you're sure of your beliefs.* Of course, it can also refer to *a jury's pronouncement of guilt.* Synonym: certitude.

Quiz 2

I. Let's review some of the words that you've seen in Groups 11–20. Match each of the following words to the correct definition or synonym on the right. If you need help, refer back to the movie excerpts and definitions. Then check the solutions on page 237.

1. Vice		A. Abhor
2. Amiable		B. Reticent
3. Loathe		C. Clemency
4. Taciturn		D. Egregious
5. Martinet		E. Iniquity
6. Absolution		F. Affable
7. Heinous		G. Propinquity
8. Temerity		H. Dogmatist
9. Cornucopia		I. Insouciant
10. Proximity		J. Audacity
11. Indifferent		K. Profusion
12. Consequences		L. Tumescent
13. Viscous		M. Insipid
14. Turgid		N. Glutinous
15. Vapid		O. Ramifications

II. Let's review several of the word parts that you've seen in Groups 11–20. Match each of the following word parts to the correct definition or synonym on the right. Then check the solutions on page 237.

16. Amicus- (as in *amicable*)		A. Not
17. Potent (as in *impotent*)		B. Foreigner
18. In- (as in *indifferent*)		C. Speak
Review:		D. Friend
19. Xeno- (as in *xenophobic*)		E. Powerful
20. Loq- (as in *loquacious*)		

III. Match each group of synonyms to its general meaning. Then check the solutions on page 237.

21. Affable   A. Hate
    Amiable
    Amicable
    Convivial
    Genial
    Gregarious
    Simpatico

22. Abhor   B. Definite
    Despise
    Detest
    Disdain
    Loathe
    Scorn

23. Categorical   C. Unconcerned
    Incontrovertible
    Indubitable
    Unconditional
    Unequivocal
    Unqualified

24. Apathetic   D. Dull
    Dispassionate
    Indifferent
    Insouciant
    Nonchalant

25. Hackneyed   E. Friendly
    Insipid
    Jejune
    Lackluster
    Pedestrian
    Trite
    Vacuous
    Vapid

Group 21

Here's an excerpt from a movie. See if you can name the movie, describe the scene, and define the boldface vocabulary words. Check your answers on the following page.

There is also a final sign-up for next week's **scholastic decathlon** competition. Chem Club president Taylor McKessie can answer all of your questions about that. (*a cell phone rings in class*) Ah, the cell phone **menace** has returned to our **crucible** of learning . . . We have zero **tolerance** for cell phones in class, so we will get to know each other in detention . . . Shall the **carnage** continue? Holidays are over people, way over!

Movie: _____

Scene: _____

_____

Scholastic might mean _____

Decathlon might mean _____

Menace might mean _____

Crucible might mean _____

Tolerance might mean _____

Carnage might mean _____

Hint: Ms. Darbus

Solutions

Let's see how you did. Check your answers and write the exact definitions. To help you memorize the vocabulary words, reread the movie excerpt or even act out the scene with a friend.

Movie: *High School Musical,* Disney Channel, 2006

Scene: Ms. Darbus (Alyson Reed) is the musical director at East High School and homeroom teacher for Troy (Zac Efron) and Gabriella (Vanessa Hudgens). She hates cell phones and is basically hilarious. She delivers these lines early in the movie when Troy and Gabriella are in homeroom.

Scholastic means *pertaining to school.* The word *school* is pretty much in the word. If half a word looks exactly like another, and you have nothing else to go on, ask yourself if they are related. Sometimes that's enough to get a feel for a word and a standardized test question correct.

Decathlon means *contest of ten events. Deca-* means *ten,* and *-athlon* means *contest.* Though a **decathlon** was originally a contest of **ten** events, it is also used now to describe any multipart contest.

Menace means *threat.* Synonyms: peril, plague.

Crucible means *place to test, change, or develop.* Calling a school a "crucible of learning" is exactly the type of overly dramatic language that makes Ms. Darbus so incredibly funny . . . and annoying. Considering her *proclivity* (tendency) for using *grandiloquent* (pompous and verbose) language, I'm surprised Ms. Darbus never used the theater word *histrionic,* which means *overly dramatic* and is a great high-level vocabulary word.

Tolerance means *leniency* or *open-mindedness,* so *"zero tolerance"* means *no leniency*—zippo. That's why anyone whose cell phone rings during Ms. Darbus' class winds up in detention. Synonyms: forbearance, indulgence.

Carnage means *slaughter.* Synonym: massacre. *Carnage* comes from the prefix *carn-,* which means *flesh,* as in *carnivorous* (flesh-eating).

Group 22

Here's an excerpt from a movie. See if you can name the movie, describe the scene, and define the boldface vocabulary words. Check your answers on the following page.

ENGLISH TEACHER: "Why, man, he doth **bestride** the narrow world like a **colossus**" might translate into "Why is he so huge and obnoxious?"

SANTA: Ha, Ha, Ha, Ho! Candy Cane–Grams!

ENGLISH TEACHER: OK, hurry up.

SANTA: Taylor Zimmerman, two for you. Glen Coco, four for you, Glen Coco! You go, Glen Coco! And, ah, Caddy Heron. Do we have a "Caddy Heron" here?

CADY: It's "Kay-dee."

SANTA: Oh "Kay-dee," here you go. One for you. And none for Gretchen Wieners. Bye.

Movie: _____

Scene: _____

_____

Bestride might mean _____

_____

Colossus might mean _____

_____

Hint: "She's totally rich because her dad invented Toaster Strudels."

Solutions

Let's see how you did. Check your answers and write the exact definitions. To help you memorize the vocabulary words, reread the movie excerpt or even act out the scene with a friend.

Movie: *Mean Girls,* Paramount Pictures, 2004

Scene: Dressed as Santa Claus, Damian (Daniel Franzese) hands out Candy Cane–Grams to his classmates at North Shore High School. The Candy Cane–Gram that Cady (Lindsay Lohan) receives says that it's from Regina (Rachel McAdams), head of the Plastics, the most popular clique at school, but Cady actually sent it to herself to "crack" Gretchen Weiners (Lacey Chabert).

Inside Scoop: Apparently, mysterious ladies' man Glenn Coco is named for a real-life friend of Tina Fey, who starred in the film and wrote the screenplay.

Bestride means *extend across* or *straddle.*

Colossus means *something or someone extremely large or important.* "Why, man, he doth **bestride** the narrow world like a **Colossus**" is from Shakespeare's *Julius Caesar*. It refers to the famous Colossus of Rhodes, one of the Seven Wonders of the Ancient World. The statue was built on the Greek island of Rhodes around 300 BCE and stood more than one hundred feet high. Even after it toppled from an earthquake, tourists visited the remains at the site for 800 years. A colossus is **very large** and the origin of the word *colossal* (very large).

Group 23

Here's an excerpt from a movie. See if you can name the movie, describe the scene, and define the boldface vocabulary words. Check your answers on the following page.

Ex-Auror, Ministry **malcontent,** and your new . . . teacher . . . (*opens a jar and takes out a spider*) Hello, my little beauty. **Engorgio!** (*The spider grows much larger.*) **Imperio!** (*makes the spider jump around the room, frightening students and making everyone laugh*) Don't worry, it's completely harmless! If she bites . . . she's lethal! Talented, isn't she? What should I have her do next? Jump out the window? (*The spider jumps toward the window, but it's closed, so the spider slams into the glass, and everyone stops laughing.*)

Movie: _____

Scene: _____

_____

Malcontent might mean _____

_____

Engorgio might mean _____

_____

Imperio might mean _____

_____

Hint: "The Yule Ball has been a tradition of the Triwizard Tournament since its **inception.** On Christmas Eve night, we and our guests gather in the Great Hall for a night of well-mannered **frivolity.**"

Solutions

Let's see how you did. Check your answers and write the exact definitions. To help you memorize the vocabulary words, reread the movie excerpt or even act out the scene with a friend.

Movie: *Harry Potter and the Goblet of Fire,* Warner Bros. Pictures, 2005

Scene: At the Hogwarts School of Witchcraft and Wizardry, Professor Mad-Eye Moody (or is it really him?) is teaching the Imperius Curse on day one of Defense Against the Dark Arts class.

Vocabulary in the Hint: *Inception* means *starting point.* Synonyms: commencement, genesis, origin. *Frivolity* means *lightheartedness.* Synonyms: gaiety, glee, jocularity, jollity, joviality, levity, merriment, mirth. Antonyms: gravitas, gravity.

Malcontent means *troublemaker. Mal-* means *badly* or *not,* so *malcontent* literally means *badly content* or *not content—dissatisfied,* which often leads to **troublemaking.** Synonym: dissident.

Engorgio looks like *engorged,* which you learned from *10 Things I Hate About You* (Group 19), and means *swollen.* Remember the synonyms, *turgid* and *tumescent?* Ms. Perky (Allison Janney) used these words in her porn novel. *Engorgio* is a spell in the *Harry Potter* series that is used to enlarge something, basically causing it to **swell.**

Imperio casts the Imperius Curse, which is one of the three Unforgivable Curses in the *Harry Potter* series. It gives the spell caster **control** over another creature, like Moody is **controlling** the engorged spider. This spell helps you remember the high-level standardized test word *imperious,* which means *bossy,* **controlling,** or *domineering.*

Group 24

Here are three excerpts from a movie. See if you can name the movie, describe the scenes, and define the boldface vocabulary words. Check your answers on the following page.

JANE: These **scruples** must seem very **provincial** to a gentleman with such elevated airs, but I do not devise these rules. I am merely obliged to obey them.

_____

JANE: **Propriety** commands me to ignorance.

_____

HENRY: Careful, Jane, Lucy's right. Mr. Lefroy does have a reputation.

JANE: Presumably as the most disagreeable, **insolent,** arrogant, **impudent, insufferable, impertinent** of men! Too many adjectives.

Movie: _____

Scenes: _____

Scruples might mean _____

Provincial might mean _____

Propriety might mean _____

Insolent might mean _____

Impudent might mean _____

Insufferable might mean _____

Impertinent might mean _____

Hint: One of the movie poster taglines for this 2007 movie is "Between _Sense and Sensibility_ and _Pride and Prejudice_ was a life worth writing about."

Solutions

Let's see how you did. Check your answers and write the exact definitions. To help you memorize the vocabulary words, reread the movie excerpts or even act out the scenes with a friend.

Movie: *Becoming Jane,* Miramax Films, 2007

Scenes: In the first thee excerpts, a young Jane Austen (Anne Hathaway) is arguing (and perhaps flirting) with Mr. Lefroy (James McAvoy). This type of *verbal sparring* (arguing) and even the vocabulary used in the film closely resemble the dialogue and vocabulary used by Jane Austen in her novels. In the fourth excerpt, Jane's brother, Henry (Joe Anderson), warns her of Lefroy's reputation as being a ladies' man. Just like the heroines in her novels, Jane is furious at Lefroy but also *enamored* (smitten) with him.

Scruples means *concerns about being immoral.* Synonyms: compunctions, qualms. *Scruples* is easy to remember if you've ever played the board game A Question of Scruples, in which players try to predict how others would react to ethical questions—would they have **concerns about being immoral?**

Provincial means *narrow* or *unsophisticated.* Synonyms: insular, parochial. Antonyms: cosmopolitan, urbane.

Propriety means *proper behavior.* Synonyms: decorum, discretion, etiquette, protocol, punctilio, rectitude, refinement.

Insolent sounds like *insulting* and means *rude.* Professor Snape often calls Harry Potter *insolent.* Synonyms: cheeky, contemptuous, contumelious, impertinent, impudent, insubordinate, pert, sassy, saucy.

Impudent means *rude.* Synonyms: cheeky, contemptuous, contumelious, impertinent, insolent, insubordinate, pert, sassy, saucy.

Insufferable means *intolerable—impossible to suffer through.*

Impertinent means *rude.* Hmm, I'm getting the feeling that Jane finds Tom a bit rude. Synonyms: cheeky, contemptuous, contumelious, impudent, insolent, insubordinate, pert, sassy, saucy.

Group 25

Here are two excerpts from a movie. See if you can name the movie, describe the scenes, and define the boldface vocabulary words. Check your answers on the following page.

Mrs. Fuller: Well, Benjamin. Might I say you are looking strikingly youthful . . . A single cane, back straight as an arrow. What **elixir** have you been drinking?

———————

Daisy: I just can't believe we're both here. Must be fate. No, what do they call it? **Kismet.**

Movie: _____

Scenes: _____

_____

Elixir might mean _____

_____

Kismet might mean _____

_____

Hint: **Benjamin:** How can I be a father when I'm heading in the other direction? . . .
Daisy: Sugar, we all end up in diapers . . .
Benjamin: I want you to have everything you want . . . I'm just not sure how to **reconcile** this.

Solutions

Let's see how you did. Check your answers and write the exact definitions. To help you memorize the vocabulary words, reread the movie excerpts or even act out the scenes with a friend.

Movie: *The Curious Case of Benjamin Button,* Paramount Pictures, 2008

Scenes: In the first excerpt, Mrs. Fuller notes that Benjamin is looking younger and then introduces him to her six-year-old granddaughter, Daisy. In the second excerpt, Daisy (Cate Blanchett) is an adult and meets an even younger-looking Benjamin (Brad Pitt) while visiting the nursing home where Benjamin grew up.

Inside Scoop: Six-year-old Daisy is played by Elle Fanning, younger sister to Dakota Fanning.

Vocabulary in the Hint: *Reconcile* means *settle* or *resolve.*

Elixir means *medicinal or magical potion,* such as one that can prolong life indefinitely.

Kismet means *fate,* something "meant to be." Synonym: providence.

Group 26

Here are two excerpts from a movie. See if you can name the movie, describe the scenes, and define the boldface vocabulary words. Check your answers on the following page.

Rose: I saw my whole life as if I had already lived it. An endless parade of parties and **cotillions,** yachts and polo matches. Always the same narrow people, the same mindless chatter. I felt like I was standing at a great **precipice,** with no one to pull me back, no one who cared or even noticed.

_____

Cal: I know you've been **melancholy.** I don't pretend to know why. I intended to save this until the engagement gala next week. But I thought tonight, perhaps as a reminder of my feelings for you . . . Fifty-six carats to be exact.

Movie: _____

Scenes: _____

_____

Cotillions might mean _____

_____

Precipice might mean _____

_____

Melancholy might mean _____

_____

Hint: "Winning that ticket, Rose, was the best thing that ever happened to me."

Solutions

Let's see how you did. Check your answers and write the exact definitions. To help you memorize the vocabulary words, reread the movie excerpts or even act out the scenes with a friend.

Movie: *Titanic,* Paramount Pictures, 1997

Scenes: Rose (Kate Winslet) feels pressured by her mother and by society into marrying Cal (Billy Zane), whom she does not love, respect, or even like. In the first excerpt, one-hundred-year-old Rose describes these feelings while relating memories of her time aboard the *Titanic* to her granddaughter (Suzy Amis) and treasure hunter Brock Lovett (Bill Paxton). In the second excerpt, Cal presents Rose with the Heart of the Ocean, a fifty-six carat diamond.

Inside Scoop: Apparently, when they first met, Kate Winslet flashed Leonardo DiCaprio to "break the ice" and make it easier to get naked in front of him later for the scene in which she poses in the nude for a portrait he's sketching.

Cotillions means *formal parties,* such as balls where *debutantes* (upper-class young women) are officially presented to society.

Precipice means *cliff.* In fact, Rose did wind up standing at a great precipice, over the bow of the ship, and Jack (Leonardo DiCaprio) pulled her back. Synonyms: bluff, crag, escarpment, scarp. Certain standardized tests like to use nature words such as these. Other examples are *bough* (tree branch), *aviary* (a place where birds are kept), *apiary* (a place where bees are kept), and *abyss* (chasm—a deep gorge or ravine).

Melancholy means *sad and gloomy.* Synonyms: atrabilious, desolate, disconsolate, doleful, dolorous, dour, forlorn, lugubrious, morose, mournful, plaintive, woebegone, wretched. Antonym: cheerful.

Group 27

Here are two excerpts from a movie. See if you can name the movie, describe the scenes, and define the boldface vocabulary words. Check your answers on the following page.

DR. HILBERT: I've devised a test. How exciting is that? Composed of twenty-three questions which I think might help uncover more truths about this narrator. Now . . . Harold, these may seem silly, but your **candor** is **paramount.**

HAROLD CRICK: OK.

DR. HILBERT: So. We know it's a woman's voice. The story involves your death. It's modern. It's in English, and I'm assuming the author has a **cursory** knowledge of the city.

_____

KAREN: How did you find me? . . . Didn't you think you were crazy?

HAROLD: Sort of. But then you were right about everything, like *everything*. And then you said, "Little did he know."

KAREN: Little did he know?

HAROLD: Yeah. It's, uh, third-person **omniscient** . . . Which meant it was someone other than me.

Movie: _____

Scenes: _____

_____

Candor might mean _____

Paramount might mean _____

Cursory might mean _____

Omniscient might mean _____

Hint: Will Ferrell plays an IRS auditor.

Solutions

Let's see how you did. Check your answers and write the exact definitions. To help you memorize the vocabulary words, reread the movie excerpts or even act out the scenes with a friend.

Movie: *Stranger than Fiction,* Columbia Pictures, 2006

Scenes: In the first excerpt, Harold (Will Ferrell) has sought out Dr. Jules Hilbert (Dustin Hoffman), an English professor, to help him understand why is hearing the voice of a woman who is narrating his life. In the second excerpt, he meets the narrator, Karen Eiffel (Emma Thompson).

Candor means *honesty*. Synonyms: bluntness, forthrightness, frankness. This word reminds me of *Candid Camera,* a TV show from the 1970s and 80s, that is the great granddaddy of all reality TV shows. The show caught people's **candid** (**honest**, unscripted) reactions to pranks. Believe it or not, my mom was on that show.

Paramount means *of supreme importance*. Synonyms: foremost, key, predominant, primary.

Cursory means *superficial and quick*. Synonyms: casual, desultory, fleeting, hasty, perfunctory.

Omniscient means *knowing everything*. *Omni-* means *all*, as in *omnipresent* (present **all-**over), and *scient-* refers to *knowing*, as in *science* (the gathering of **knowledge**), so *omniscient* means *all-knowing—knowing everything*. The narrator is **omniscient**—she **knows everything** about Harold. *Third-person omniscient* is a style of writing in which the narrator **knows everything,** including characters' thoughts, as opposed to *first-person* writing in which the narrator uses "I" and can only describe his or her own thoughts, assumptions, and observations.

Group 28

Here's an excerpt from a movie. See if you can name the movie, describe the scene, and define the boldface vocabulary word. Check your answers on the following page.

CLAIRE: (*about her sister, Gloria, planning to marry Jeremy*) I can't believe that they're getting married. I mean, don't you think that's really soon?

SECRETARY CLEARY: Well, you know Gloria, she's **impetuous,** has to have what she wants when she wants it. We had to give her a Sweet Sixteen on her thirteenth birthday. You remember that.

Movie: _____

Scene: _____

_____

Impetuous might mean _____

_____

Hint: Gloria is played by Isla Fisher, who starred in *Confessions of a Shopaholic; Definitely, Maybe;* and *Hot Rod.*

Solutions

Let's see how you did. Check your answers and write the exact definition. To help you memorize the vocabulary word, reread the movie excerpt or even act out the scene with a friend.

Movie: *Wedding Crashers* (Uncorked Edition), New Line Cinema, 2005

Scene: Secretary Cleary (Christopher Walken) and his daughter, Claire (Rachel McAdams), are walking in a market looking at flowers for Claire's wedding to Zach (Bradley Cooper), whom she does not truly want to marry. That's why she's so hesitant about Gloria's (Isla Fisher) marrying Jeremy (Vince Vaughn).

Inside Scoop: Christopher Walken and Rachel McAdams had to film so many takes of their dance scene that it got pretty dull and hard to keep smiling, so Walken occasionally whispered "fart" to keep McAdams laughing during the scene.

Impetuous means *spontaneous and impulsive.* Synonyms: hasty, heedless, imprudent, precipitate, rash, temerarious, unpremeditated.

Group 29

Here are two excerpts from a movie. See if you can name the movie, describe the scenes, and define the boldface vocabulary words. Check your answers on the following page.

CLEMENTINE: (*about her blue hair dye*) Anyway, this company makes a whole line of colors with equally snappy names: red **menace**, yellow fever, green revolution . . .

JOEL: (*about Clementine's name*) It's a pretty name though. It really is nice. It means *merciful*, right, ***clemency?***

CLEMENTINE: Although it hardly fits. I'm a **vindictive** little bitch, truth be told.

———————

CARRIE: What can I say, Joel? You know Clementine; she's like that. She's **impulsive**. She decided to erase you almost as a **lark**.

Movie: _____

Scenes: _____

_____

Menace might mean _____

Clemency might mean _____

Vindictive might mean _____

Impulsive might mean _____

Lark might mean _____

Hint: "There's an emotional core to each of our memories, and when you **eradicate** that core, it starts its **degradation** process. By the time you wake up in the morning, all the memories we've targeted will have withered and disappeared as in a dream upon waking."

Solutions

Let's see how you did. Check your answers and write the exact definitions. To help you memorize the vocabulary words, reread the movie excerpts or even act out the scenes with a friend.

Movie: *Eternal Sunshine of the Spotless Mind,* Focus Features, 2004

Scenes: The first excerpt is from the *poignant* (touching) scene at the beginning of the film in which Joel (Jim Carrey) and Clementine (Kate Winslet) meet after having erased each other from their memories (in this film, characters can undergo a procedure to erase painful memories from their minds). In the third excerpt, a friend is consoling Joel after he's been "erased" by Clementine.

Inside Scoop: The title of this film is taken from a poem by English poet Alexander Pope:

How happy is the blameless *vestal's* lot!
The world forgetting, by the world forgot.
Eternal sunshine of the spotless mind!
Each pray'r accepted, and each wish resign'd . . .

Vestal means *virgin* or *pure and chaste (nonsexual) person.*

Vocabulary in the Hint: *Eradicate* means *erase completely.* Synonym: expunge. *Degradation* means *deterioration.* Synonym: atrophy. *Degradation* can also mean *humiliation.*

Menace means *threat.* Synonyms: peril, plague.

Clemency means *mercy.* Synonyms: forbearance, leniency.

Vindictive means *revengeful.* Synonym: malevolent, malicious, spiteful, rancorous, vengeful.

Impulsive means *spontaneous.* Synonyms: hasty, heedless, impetuous, imprudent, precipitate, rash, temerarious, unpremeditated. You learned *impetuous* from the *Wedding Crashers* scene in Group 28.

Lark means *an unplanned or mischievous bit of amusement.* Synonyms: escapade, jape, prank, whim.

Group 30

Here are three excerpts from a movie. See if you can name the movie, describe the scenes, and define the boldface vocabulary words. Check your answers on the following page.

GRACIE: Just hear me out . . . I really feel that the situation bears further **scrutiny** and our continued presence here at the pageant.

_____

VICTOR: A sniveling, **obsequious** weasel of a human being.

ERIC: You know her son?

VICTOR: So do you. It's Frank . . . His name's Morningside. He changed it to cover his many **indiscretions.**

ERIC: Wait a minute, how do you know that?

VICTOR: I have been around this pageant for many years. I could shock you with the intimate details I am **privy to.**

_____

VICTOR: Agent Mathews! Gracie! Thank God you're still here. There's been an emergency at the farewell breakfast. Somebody's found some sort of an **incendiary** device. Come on. Quickly.

Movie: _____

Scenes: _____

Scrutiny might mean _____

Obsequious might mean _____

Indiscretions might mean _____

Privy to might mean _____

Incendiary might mean _____

Hint: Sandra Bullock

Solutions

Let's see how you did. Check your answers and write the exact definitions. To help you memorize the vocabulary words, reread the movie excerpts or even act out the scenes with a friend.

Movie: *Miss Congeniality,* Warner Bros., 2000

Scenes: In the first excerpt, FBI agent Gracie (Sandra Bullock) is trying to convince her boss not to close their investigation of a terrorist threat at the Miss United States beauty pageant. In the second excerpt, Victor (Michael Caine), a beauty pageant coach, tells Eric (Benjamin Bratt), an FBI agent, that Frank is actually Kathy's (Candice Bergen) son. In the third excerpt, Victor pretends there is an emergency to lure Gracie to a surprise ceremony where she is crowned Miss Congeniality.

Scrutiny means *close examination*. Synonym: probing.

Obsequious means *excessively flattering or obedient,* like a "brownnoser" or "suck-up." The way Wormtail acts toward Lord Voldemort in the *Harry Potter* series is a perfect example of **obsequious** behavior. Synonyms: fawning, ingratiating, oleaginous, servile, sycophantic, toady. I've seen almost every one of these words on standardized tests. Learn them and you'll gain points!

Indiscretions means *sinful or unwise actions*. Synonyms for *indiscretion:* impropriety, imprudence, injudiciousness, peccadillo, solecism, transgression.

Privy to means *in on* or *aware of*. Synonym: cognizant of.

Incendiary means *designed to cause fire or conflict,* like the spell *Incendio* from the *Harry Potter* series, which sends **flames** bursting out of the spellcaster's wand. Synonyms: combustible, flammable, seditious.

Quiz 3

I. Let's review some of the words that you've seen in Groups 21–30. Match each of the following words to the correct definition or synonym on the right. If you need help, refer back to the movie excerpts and definitions. Then check the solutions on page 237.

1. Malcontent		A. Insular
2. Provincial		B. Impudent
3. Insipid		C. Decorum
4. Insolent		D. Dissident
5. Propriety		E. Morose
6. Kismet		F. Pedestrian
7. Precipice		G. Desultory
8. Melancholy		H. Temerarious
9. Candor		I. Providence
10. Cursory		J. Bluff
11. Omniscient		K. Close examination
12. Impetuous		L. Sycophantic
13. Clemency		M. Forbearance
14. Scrutiny		N. Frankness
15. Obsequious		O. All-knowing

II. Let's review several of the word parts that you've seen in Groups 21–30. Match each of the following word parts to the correct definition or synonym on the right. Then check the solutions on page 237.

16. Deca- (as in *decagon*)	A. Friend
17. -athlon (as in *decathlon*)	B. Powerful
18. Mal- (as in *malcontent*)	C. All
19. Omni- (as in *omnipresent*)	D. Badly, not
Review:	E. Ten
20. Amicus- (as in *amicable*)	F. Contest
21. Potent (as in *impotent*)	

III. Match each group of synonyms to its general meaning. Then check the solutions on page 237.

22. Insular
    Parochial
    Provincial

    A. Dull

23. Hackneyed
    Insipid
    Jejune
    Lackluster
    Pedestrian
    Trite
    Vacuous
    Vapid

    B. Excessively obedient

24. Cheeky
    Contemptuous
    Contumelious
    Impertinent
    Impudent
    Insolent
    Insubordinate
    Pert
    Sassy
    Saucy

    C. Unsophisticated

25. Fawning
    Ingratiating
    Obsequious
    Oleaginous
    Servile
    Sycophantic
    Toady

    D. Rude

Here are two excerpts from a movie. See if you can name the movie, describe the scenes, and define the boldface vocabulary words. Check your answers on the following page.

TIBBY: My Carma-poochie-ay, I'm writing from the post office, and this express mail costs more than I make in two hours at Wallmans, so these jeans better get to you tomorrow. (*flashback to Tibby interviewing young girls at a lemonade stand*) Here we are on a typical Bethesda corner where generations of young **entrepreneurs** have proved the old **adage** "when life hands you lemons, make lemonade."

DRESSMAKER: Usually a roughly constructed **prototype** works as a starting point, but in this case . . . We will fix the hem on Krista's, and we will start over on the other one.

CARMEN: Carmen! The other one's name, it's Carmen!

Movie: _____

Scenes: _____

_____

Entrepreneurs might mean _____

_____

Adage might mean _____

_____

Prototype might mean _____

_____

Hint: "Magic has come to us in a pair of pants."

Solutions

Let's see how you did. Check your answers and write the exact definitions. To help you memorize the vocabulary words, reread the movie excerpts or even act out the scenes with a friend.

Movie: *The Sisterhood of the Traveling Pants,* Warner Bros., 2005

Scenes: In the first excerpt, Tibby (Amber Tamblyn) is at the post office mailing the blue jeans to her friend, Carmen (America Ferrera), and describing the events of the previous week. In the second excerpt, Carmen is at a dressmaker with her father's fiancée to get fitted for her bridesmaid dress, but the dress is way too small and she feels self-conscious and hurt.

Entrepreneurs means *self-employed business people.*

Adage means *a saying* or *short and memorable statement of truth.* Synonyms: aphorism, apothegm, axiom, dictum, epigram, maxim, precept, proverb, saw, truism.

Prototype means *first model or typical example of something. Proto-* means *first,* as in *protozoan (single-celled organism,* named for being the **first** animal). Synonyms: archetype, epitome, exemplar, paradigm, paragon, quintessence, template.

Group 32

Here are three excerpts from a movie. See if you can name the movie, describe the scenes, and define the boldface vocabulary words. Check your answers on the following page.

REPORTER: Mia Thermopolis is the daughter of local **eclectic** artist, Helen Thermopolis. They currently live in a refurbished firehouse south of Market Street. Mia is also the only grandchild of Queen Clarisse Renaldi, whose husband, King Rupert, passed away last year.

QUEEN: Philippe knew that my firstborn, his brother Pierre, wanted to **abdicate,** which he did eventually, to join the church.

QUEEN: With the power vested in me by the Royal Crown of Genovia, I dub thee, Arthur Washington, and I dub thee, Bruce Macintosh, Masters of the Order of the Rose. And all of you bear witness to this **auspicious** moment in history. (*to Arthur and Bruce*) Please rise.

Movie: _____

Scenes: _____

_____

Eclectic might mean _____

_____

Abdicate might mean _____

_____

Auspicious might mean _____

_____

Hint: This was Anne Hathaway's first movie.

Solutions

Let's see how you did. Check your answers and write the exact definitions. To help you memorize the vocabulary words, reread the movie excerpts or even act out the scenes with a friend.

Movie: *The Princess Diaries*, Walt Disney Pictures, 2001

Scenes: In the first excerpt, Mia's (Anne Hathaway) hairdresser has outed her to the press, who is waiting for her to arrive at her school. In the second excerpt, Queen Clarisse Renaldi (Julie Andrews) explains why Mia's father chose to return home to Genovia to become a prince. In the third excerpt, in order to prevent Mia from being arrested for driving without a license, the Queen bestows the Order of the Rose on a policeman and a trolley driver.

Inside Scoop: Mandy Moore's first major acting role is in this movie. She plays head cheerleader Lana Thomas.

Eclectic means *from varied sources*. The reporter means that Mia's mom is an artist whose artistic style draws upon **various sources**. Synonyms: disparate, heterogeneous, manifold, motley, multifarious, myriad, sundry.

Abdicate means *give up one's office*. Synonyms: abjure, cede, demit, disclaim, forsake, relinquish, renounce, repudiate, resign, retire, vacate.

Auspicious means *fortunate*. Synonyms: felicitous, opportune, propitious, providential.

Here are two excerpts from a movie. See if you can name the movie, describe the scenes, and define the boldface vocabulary words. Check your answers on the following pages.

ENGLISH TEACHER: What did everyone think of *The Sun Also Rises?*

STUDENT: I loved it. He's so romantic.

KAT: Romantic? Hemingway? He was an abusive, alcoholic **misogynist** who **squandered** half of his life . . .

JOEY: As opposed to a bitter, **self-righteous** hag who has no friends . . .

PATRICK: (*enters class late*) What did I miss?

KAT: The **oppressive, patriarchal** values that dictate our education.

PATRICK: Good. (*leaves the room*)

CAMERON: You OK?

MICHAEL: Yeah, just a minor encounter with the **shrew.** (*points to Kat*) That's your girlfriend's sister.

CAMERON: Wait, *that's* Bianca's sister?

MICHAEL: The muling, **rampallion wretch,** herself.

Movie: _____

Scenes: _____

_____

Hint: "How do I **loathe** thee? Let me count the ways."

Misogynist might mean _____

_____

Squandered might mean _____

_____

Self-righteous might mean _____

_____

Oppressive might mean _____

_____

Patriarchal might mean _____

_____

Shrew might mean _____

_____

Rampallion might mean _____

_____

Wretch might mean _____

_____

Solutions

Let's see how you did. Check your answers and write the exact definitions. To help you memorize the vocabulary words, reread the movie excerpts or even act out the scenes with a friend.

Movie: *10 Things I Hate About You,* Touchstone Pictures, 1999

Scenes: Early in the movie, Kat (Julia Stiles) discusses Ernest Hemingway in her high-school English class, while Patrick (Heath Ledger) shows up late for class. In the second excerpt, Michael (David Krumholtz) introduces Cameron (Joseph Gordon-Levitt) to Kat.

Inside Scoop: Cameron is played by a very young Joseph Gordon-Levitt, now famous as Tom from *(500) Days of Summer!*

Vocabulary in the Hint: *Loathe* means *hate.* Synonyms: abhor, condemn, despise, detest, disdain, execrate, scorn. Antonym: love.

Solutions (continued)

Misogynist means *hater of women*. *Gyn-* refers to *women* (which is why a doctor who specializes in women's reproductive health is called a **gyn**ecologist).

Squandered means *wasted.*

Self-righteous means *with a superior attitude*. Standardized tests love the synonym *sanctimonious*.

Oppressive means *harsh and constraining*. Synonyms: autocratic, despotic, dictatorial, draconian, repressive, tyrannical, undemocratic. Antonyms: humane, lenient.

Patriarchal means *controlled by men*. The word part *-arch* refers to *ruler*, as in *monarchy* (*mono-* means *one*, so *monarchy* means *rule by one*—usually by a king or queen), *oligarchy* (*oligo-* means *a small number*, so *oligarchy* means *rule by a small group of individuals*), *matriarchy* (rule by women), and *plutarchy* (rule by the wealthy).

Shrew means *small mouse-like animal*, or, as it is used in this case, *bad-tempered woman*. Synonyms: termagant, virago.

Rampallion means *scoundrelous*. This is a word Shakespeare used that you don't see too much anymore—though I've seen the SAT occasionally pull out exactly this kind of *obsolete* (outdated) word for the most difficult questions. Synonym: fustilarian.

Wretch means *unhappy or wicked person*. Synonyms: miscreant, picaroon, reprobate, rogue, scoundrel.

Group 34

Here are two excerpts from a movie. See if you can name the movie, describe the scenes, and define the boldface vocabulary words. Check your answers on the following page.

Eric: Women are **mercurial,** man.

Brad: And you did just start dating last week.

James: It was eleven days ago.

Eric: You didn't tell her about the scarlet V, did you?

James: That has nothing to do with it.

———————

Sue: I told my brother we made out . . . He told my parents . . . We're Catholic . . . (*apologetic*) Pete told my parents that you're Jewish.

Joel: Oh, but I'm an **atheist,** maybe more of a **pragmatic nihilist** I guess, or an **existential pagan** if you will . . .

Movie: _____

Scenes: _____

_____

Mercurial might mean _____

Atheist might mean _____

Pragmatic might mean _____

Nihilist might mean _____

Existential might mean _____

Pagan might mean _____

Hint: Never ever let anyone win a giant-ass panda, and *definitely* don't eat the corn dogs!

Solutions

Let's see how you did. Check your answers and write the exact definitions. To help you memorize the vocabulary words, reread the movie excerpts or even act out the scenes with a friend.

Movie: *Adventureland,* Miramax Films, 2009

Scenes: In the first excerpt, James (Jesse Eisenberg) is talking with his college friends after his girlfriend broke up with him. The "scarlet V" refers to the fact that he's a virgin (he's waiting for the right person). In the second excerpt, Sue tells Joel that she can't date him because he's Jewish, for which Emily (Kristen Stewart) reams her out.

Inside Scoop: If you haven't seen this movie, you should. It's by the director of *Superbad,* and it features Kristen Stewart, Ryan Reynolds, Martin Starr, Bill Hader, Jesse Eisenberg, and Kristen Wiig!

Mercurial means *unpredictable* or *quickly changing.* To help you remember this word, think of the planet Mercury, the fastest moving planet. You can see the connection between **moving fast** and **quickly changing.** Synonyms: capricious, erratic, fickle, fluctuating, impulsive, inconstant, labile, mutable, protean, temperamental, volatile, whimsical. Antonym: stable.

Atheist means *a person who believes that there is no God. A-* means *not* or *without* and *theist* comes from *theos* meaning *God,* so *atheist* means *without God.*

Pragmatic means *practical.* Antonym: idealistic.

Nihilist refers to *a person who rejects religion and believes that life is meaningless.* It comes from *nihil-,* which means *nothing,* as in *nil* (nothing) and *annihilate* (destroy—reduce to **nothing**).

Existential refers to *the belief that each person must find his or her own meaning to existence.*

Pagan means *not Jewish or Christian.* Joel's response, ". . . I'm an **atheist,** maybe more of a **pragmatic nihilist** I guess, or an **existential pagan** if you will" is probably not gonna get Sue to make out with him anytime soon.

Group 35

Here's an excerpt from a movie. See if you can name the movie, describe the scene, and define the boldface vocabulary word. Check your answers on the following page.

GILDEROY LOCKHART: Can you possibly imagine a better way to serve detention than by helping me to answer my fan mail? . . . Fame is a **fickle** friend . . . Celebrity is as celebrity does. Remember that.

Movie: _____

Scene: _____

_____

Fickle might mean _____

_____

Hint: "Flagrate!" "Lumos!"

Solutions

Let's see how you did. Check your answers and write the exact definition. To help you memorize the vocabulary word, reread the movie excerpt or even act out the scene with a friend.

Movie: *Harry Potter and the Chamber of Secrets,* Warner Bros. Pictures, 2002

Scene: Gilderoy Lockhart (Kenneth Branagh), the new Defense Against the Dark Arts teacher at Hogwarts School of Witchcraft and Wizardry, dispenses his questionable wisdom to Harry Potter (Daniel Radcliffe).

Vocabulary in the Hint: In the *Harry Potter* series, *Lumos* is the spell for light; basically, it turns the caster's wand into a flashlight. *Lumos* comes from *lumin-,* meaning *light,* as in *luminous* (radiant) and *luminary* (a person who en**light**ens and inspires others). *Flagrate* is the spell that casts a glowing, fiery mark, such as Hermione uses on doors in the Department of Mysteries in *Harry Potter and the Order of the Phoenix. Flagrate* helps you remember high-level vocabulary words such as *conflagration* (fire).

Fickle means *unpredictable* or *changing too easily,* just like *mercurial* from *Adventureland* in Group 34. In *New Moon,* when Bella and Edward are discussing *Romeo and Juliet,* Edward calls Romeo *fickle* since he was in love with Rosaline but then **quickly** fell for Juliet. Synonyms: capricious, erratic, impetuous, mercurial, vacillating, whimsical.

Here are two excerpts from a movie. See if you can name the movie, describe the scenes, and define the boldface vocabulary words. Check your answers on the following page.

B.S.: I've never given much thought to how I would die. But dying in the place of someone I love seems like a good way to go. So, I can't bring myself to regret the decision to leave home. I would miss Phoenix; I would miss the heat; I would miss my loving, **erratic, harebrained** mother and her new husband.

E.C.: Alice's visions are **subjective.** I mean the future can always change.

Movie: _____

Scenes: _____

_____

Erratic might mean _____

_____

Harebrained might mean _____

_____

Subjective might mean _____

_____

Hint: "Hey, did you get contacts? . . . Your eyes were black the last time I saw you, and now they're like **golden-brown.**"

Solutions

Let's see how you did. Check your answers and write the exact definitions. To help you memorize the vocabulary words, reread the movie excerpts or even act out the scenes with a friend.

Movie: *Twilight,* Summit Entertainment, 2008

Scenes: The first excerpt is of Bella's (Kristen Stewart) classic opening lines in *Twilight*. In the second excerpt, Edward (Robert Pattinson) describes Alice's (Ashley Greene) unique ability to foresee the future.

Vocabulary in the Hint: In the biology class scene, you get your first close-up of Edward's famous golden-brown eyes. In the *Twilight* books, Stephenie Meyer also calls them *ocher, topaz,* and *tawny*— high-level synonyms for *golden-brown*. Another synonym is *fulvous,* but she left that one out; I don't think it would be quite as sexy to stare into Edward's **fulvous** eyes. By the way, did you notice Stephenie Meyer's *cameo* (small role) in the film? In the second diner scene, a bit more than an hour into the film, Stephenie Meyer is sitting at the counter working on a laptop and the waitress says, "Here's your veggie plate, Stephenie."

Erratic means *inconsistent and unpredictable*. Bella always speaks of her mom as childlike and erratic. In the book, she says, "How could I leave my loving, erratic, harebrained mother to fend for herself?" Synonyms: arbitrary, capricious, fickle, impetuous, mercurial, sporadic. Quiz: For each of the following movies, name a synonym from the above list that was in an excerpt from that movie: *Clueless, Adventureland, Harry Potter and the Chamber of Secrets,* and *Wedding Crashers?* Answer: *Clueless*—sporadic, *Adventureland*—mercurial, *Harry Potter and the Chamber of Secrets*—fickle, *Wedding Crashers*—impetuous.

Harebrained means *silly* or *foolish,* and implies that a person has the same size brain as a *hare* (rabbit). So, I suppose a person who is bird-brained is even more foolish. Synonyms: crackpot, ditzy, flaky, impracticable, madcap, rash, reckless, scatterbrained.

Subjective means *based on a person's own ideas,* as opposed to *objective,* which means *based on facts, rather than a person's own ideas.* Edward means that Alice's visions are **subject to people's plans and ideas.** Bella uses this very fact to get around Alice's visions throughout the *Twilight* saga books and movies.

Group 37

Here are three excerpts from a movie. See if you can name the movie, describe the scenes, and define the boldface vocabulary words. Check your answers on the following page.

MANNY: And so, in the end, the little burro reached his mommy, and they lived happily ever after . . .

YOUNG ELK: *Burro* is a **demeaning** name. Technically, it's called a *wild ass*.

MANNY: Fine. The wild ass boy came home to his wild ass mother. (*The young animals all laugh.*)

—————————

AARDVARK: (*questioning Manny*) Say, buddy, not to **cast aspersions on** your survival instincts or nothing, but haven't mammoths pretty much gone extinct?

—————————

(*Eddie and Crash are taunting Diego.*)

DIEGO: Big mistake, you **miscreants**!

EDDIE: Miscreants? (*Eddie and Crash laugh.*)

SID: Uh, Diego, they're possums.

Movie: _____

Scenes: _____

_____

Demeaning might mean _____

Cast aspersions on might mean _____

Miscreants might mean _____

Hint: Things are melting down.

Solutions

Let's see how you did. Check your answers and write the exact definitions. To help you memorize the vocabulary words, reread the movie excerpts or even act out the scenes with a friend.

Movie: *Ice Age: The Meltdown,* 20th Century Fox, 2006

Scenes: In the first excerpt, Manny the mammoth (voiced by Ray Romano) has just finished telling a story to a group of young animals. In the second excerpt, an aardvark points out that mammoths are *extinct* (no longer existing), and in the third excerpt, possums Eddie and Crash (voiced by Josh Peck and Seann William Scott, respectively) are taunting Diego the saber-toothed tiger (voiced by Denis Leary), which, for your reference, is never a very good idea.

Demeaning means *humiliating*. Synonyms: degrading, ignominious, inglorious.

Cast aspersions on means *insultingly criticize*. Synonyms: belittle, decry, defame, denigrate, denounce, disparage, impugn, libel, malign, pillory, slander, vilify.

Miscreants means *villains*. Synonyms: malefactors, malfeasants, picaroons, reprobates, rogues, scoundrels.

Here's an excerpt from a movie. See if you can name the movie, describe the scene, and define the boldface vocabulary words. Check your answers on the following page.

J.: My only love sprung from my only hate! Too early seen unknown, and known too late! **Prodigious** birth of love it is to me, that I must love a **loathed** enemy.

Movie: _____

Scene: _____

_____

Prodigious might mean _____

_____

Loathed might mean _____

_____

Hint: "Two households both alike in dignity, in fair Verona where we lay our scene . . . From forth the fatal loins of these two foes, a pair of star-crossed lovers take their life."

Solutions

Let's see how you did. Check your answers and write the exact definitions. To help you memorize the vocabulary words, reread the movie excerpt or even act out the scene with a friend.

Movie: *William Shakespeare's Romeo + Juliet,* 20th Century Fox, 1996

Scene: In this excerpt, Juliet Capulet (Claire Danes) declares her love for Romeo Montague (Leonardo DiCaprio) right before the famous "Romeo, Romeo where fore art thou, Romeo" balcony scene. This film is a must-see oldie. You've got Leonardo at his best, plus a few surprises including a very young Paul Rudd and, in drag, Harold Perrineau (who played Michael Dawson on *Lost*)! Plus every time Tybalt (John Leguizamo) speaks, I can't help but picture *Ice Age*'s Sid the sloth!

Prodigious means *enormous* or *amazing*. Synonyms: colossal, inordinate, mammoth, wondrous. Juliet means that the "birth of love" she feels for Romeo is so **enormous** that she cannot fight it or ignore it, even though Romeo is her family's enemy.

Loathed means *hated*. Synonyms: abhorred, despised, detested, disdained, execrated, scorned.

Group 39

Here's an excerpt from a movie. See if you can name the movie, describe the scene, and define the boldface vocabulary words. Check your answers on the following page.

‖‖

S.T.: All right! You, sir? How about a shave? . . . You, sir! Too, sir. Welcome to the grave. I will have **vengeance.** I will have **salvation.** Who, sir? You, sir! No one's in the chair. Come on, come on! . . . You, sir? Anybody? Gentlemen, now don't be shy. Not one man, no, nor ten men, nor a hundred can **assuage** me. I will have you! And I will get him back even as he **gloats.** In the meantime, I'll practice on less honorable throats. And my Lucy lies in ashes, and I'll never see my girl again. But the work waits! I'm alive at last, and I'm full of joy!

‖‖

Movie: _____

Scene: _____

_____

Vengeance might mean _____

_____

Salvation might mean _____

_____

Assuage might mean _____

_____

Gloats might mean _____

_____

Hint: "It take-a **panache,** it take-a da passion for da art, to shave-a da face, to trim-a da beard . . . "

Solutions

Let's see how you did. Check your answers and write the exact definitions. To help you memorize the vocabulary words, reread the movie excerpt or even act out the scene with a friend.

Movie: *Sweeney Todd: The Demon Barber of Fleet Street,* DreamWorks, 2007

Scene: This excerpt is from a song that Sweeney Todd (Johnny Depp) sings called "Epiphany." *Epiphany* means *sudden realization of great truth.* Sweeney Todd is a barber who is falsely imprisoned by Judge Turpin (Alan Rickman), who wants to steal Todd's wife. Sweeney has a **sudden realization** that until he can get revenge on Turpin, he will vent his anger on other customers.

Inside Scoop: Did you recognize Sacha Baron Cohen, a.k.a. Borat, a.k.a. Ali G, a.k.a. Brüno, as Sweeney's competitor, Adolfo Pirelli? Of all Sacha Baron Cohen's many personas, Pirelli reminds me most of Cohen's character Jean Girard from *Talladega Nights*.

Vocabulary in the Hint: *Panache* means *flair.* Synonym: élan.

Vengeance means *revenge.* Synonyms: reprisal, requital, retaliation, vindication.

Salvation means *being saved.* Synonyms: deliverance, redemption.

Assuage means *soothe* or *satisfy*. Synonyms: allay, alleviate, ameliorate, conciliate, mollify, pacify, palliate, placate. This is one of the SAT's favorite sets of synonyms. You'll see at least one of these words on almost every SAT.

Gloats means *brags about one's good fortune or about the misfortune of others.* Synonyms: boasts, swaggers.

Group 40

Here are two excerpts from a movie. See if you can name the movie, describe the scenes, and define the boldface vocabulary words. Check your answers on the following page.

ROSE: . . . the **inertia** of my life, plunging ahead, and me powerless to stop it . . .

JACK: Do you love him?

ROSE: Pardon me?

JACK: Do you love him?

ROSE: You're being very rude . . . You are rude and **uncouth** and **presumptuous** and I am leaving now.

———————

CAL: Rose and I differ somewhat in our definition of fine art. Not to **impugn** your work, sir.

Movie: _____

Scenes: _____

Inertia might mean _____

_____

Uncouth might mean _____

_____

Presumptuous might mean _____

_____

Impugn might mean _____

_____

Hint: "I'm the king of the world!"

Solutions

Let's see how you did. Check your answers and write the exact definitions. To help you memorize the vocabulary words, reread the movie excerpts or even act out the scenes with a friend.

Movie: *Titanic,* Paramount Pictures, 1997

Scenes: In the first excerpt, Rose (Kate Winslet) describes to Jack Dawson (Leonardo DiCaprio) that she feels pressured by her mother and by society. In response, he asks if she loves Cal (Billy Zane), whom she is arranged to marry. In the second excerpt, Jack is eating dinner at Cal and Rose's table on the first-class deck. Rose tells everyone that Jack is an artist, and since Cal is jealous, he insults both Jack and Rose.

Inside Scoop: Gaelic Storm is the real-life band that plays when Rose and Jack dance at the lively party on the third-class deck.

Inertia means *the tendency for things to continue along the path they are on.*

Uncouth means *lacking polite manners.* Synonyms: boorish, indecorous, loutish, plebeian, unrefined.

Presumptuous means *presuming too much—overly bold.* Synonyms: audacious, brazen, impertinent, impudent.

Impugn means *challenge.* In fact, the root *pug-* usually implies *fight* or *challenge,* such as *pugnacious* (quick to fight) and *pugilist* (a boxer).

Quiz 4

I. Let's review some of the words that you've seen in Groups 31–40. Match each of the following words to the correct definition or synonym on the right. If you need help, refer back to the movie excerpts and definitions. Then check the solutions on page 237.

1. Adage	A. Opportune
2. Prototype	B. Motley
3. Eclectic	C. Sanctimonious
4. Abdicate	D. Maxim
5. Auspicious	E. Exemplar
6. Self-righteous	F. Ameliorate
7. Fickle	G. Abjure
8. Demeaning	H. Challenge
9. Prodigious	I. Audacious
10. Loathe	J. Degrading
11. Assuage	K. Colossal
12. Presumptuous	L. Capricious
13. Uncouth	M. Boasts
14. Impugn	N. Abhor
15. Gloats	O. Boorish

II. Let's review several of the word parts that you've seen in Groups 31–40. Match each of the following word parts to the correct definition or synonym on the right. Then check the solutions on page 237.

16. -Arch (as in *patriarch*)	A. One
17. Mono- (as in *monarch*)	B. Light
18. Gyn- (as in *gynecologist*)	C. Ruler
19. Lumin- (as in *luminous*)	D. Fight
20. Pug- (as in *pugnacious*)	E. Women

III. Match each group of synonyms to its general meaning. Then check the solutions on page 237.

21. Adage   A. Unpredictable
    Aphorism
    Apothegm
    Axiom
    Epigram
    Maxim
    Precept
    Proverb
    Saw
    Truism

22. Disparate   B. A saying
    Eclectic
    Heterogeneous
    Motley
    Multifarious

23. Auspicious   C. Hate
    Felicitous
    Opportune
    Propitious
    Providential

24. Capricious   D. Varied
    Erratic
    Fickle
    Impetuous
    Mercurial
    Vacillating
    Whimsical

25. Abhor   E. Fortunate
    Detest
    Execrate
    Loathe

Group 41

Here are two excerpts from a movie. See if you can name the movie, describe the scenes, and define the boldface vocabulary words. Check your answers on the following page.

PRIME MINISTER'S AIDE: This is our first really important test. Let's take a stand.

PRIME MINISTER: Right. Right. I understand that, but I have decided not to, not this time. We will, of course, try to be clever, but . . . I'm not going to act like a **petulant** child.

PRIME MINISTER: Natalie, I'm starting to feel uncomfortable about us working in such close **proximity** every day and me knowing so little about you. It seems **elitist** and wrong.

NATALIE: Well, there's not much to know . . .

PRIME MINISTER: And, ah, you live with your husband, ah, boyfriend . . .

NATALIE: No, I just split up with my boyfriend actually, so I'm back with my Mum and Dad for a while.

Movie: _____

Scenes: _____

_____

Petulant might mean _____

_____

Proximity might mean _____

_____

Elitist might mean _____

_____

Hint: "Love actually is all around."

Solutions

Let's see how you did. Check your answers and write the exact definitions. To help you memorize the vocabulary words, reread the movie excerpts or even act out the scenes with a friend.

Movie: *Love Actually,* Universal Pictures, 2003

Scenes: In the first excerpt, the British Prime Minister (Hugh Grant) is speaking with his cabinet about his upcoming meeting with the President of the United States. In the second excerpt, the Prime Minister has a crush on Natalie (Martine McCutcheon), a member of his staff, and is trying to find out if she has a boyfriend.

Petulant means *irritable*. Synonyms: cantankerous, churlish, curmudgeonly, fractious, irascible, peevish, querulous, sullen. *Querulous* is easy to remember because it sounds like having a *quarrel* (angry disagreement), and I remember *peevish* by thinking of Peeves, the **irritable** and mischievous *poltergeist* (disruptive ghost) in the *Harry Potter* books and movies.

Proximity means *nearness*. You learned this word from *High School Musical*'s Ms. Darbus in Group 15. Synonym: propinquity.

Elitist means *snobbishly favoring the wealthy or powerful*. The Prime Minister means that he does not want to act like a **powerful person who ignores his staff,** although really he's just trying to find out whether Natalie has a boyfriend so he can ask her out.

Group 42

Here's an excerpt from a movie. See if you can name the movie, describe the scene, and define the boldface vocabulary words. Check your answers on the following page.

I'm merely remarking upon the **paradox** of asking a masked man who he is . . . But on this most **auspicious** of nights, permit me then, **in lieu of** the more commonplace **sobriquet,** to suggest the character of this *dramatis personae* . . . **Verily,** this **vichyssoise** of **verbiage veers** most **verbose,** so let me simply add that it's my very good honor to meet you, and you may call me . . .

Movie: _____

Scene: _____

_____

Paradox might mean _____

Auspicious might mean _____

In lieu of might mean _____

Sobriquet might mean _____

Dramatis personae might mean _____

Verily might mean _____

Vichyssoise might mean _____

Verbiage might mean _____

Veers might mean _____

Verbose might mean _____

Hint: All the "v" words should give this one away.

Solutions

Let's see how you did. Check your answers and write the exact definitions. To help you memorize the vocabulary words, reread the movie excerpt or even act out the scene with a friend.

Movie: *V for Vendetta,* Warner Bros., 2006

Scene: This film, based on a graphic novel, is set in the future in London. The film tells the story of a freedom fighter, called V. In the excerpt, V (Hugo Weaving) meets Evey (Natalie Portman) in a dark alley where three members of the government's secret police are harassing her. V saves her and begins his legendary introduction, to which she replies, "Are you like a crazy person?"

Paradox means *contradictory statement.*

Auspicious means *likely to bring good fortune.* Synonyms: felicitous, opportune, propitious, providential.

In lieu of means *in place of.*

Sobriquet means *nickname.*

Dramatis personae means *participants* and translates from Latin as *persons of the drama.*

Verily means *truly,* and, in fact, *veri-* means *truth* as in *verify* (check the **truth** of—confirm), *verity* (**truth**), *verisimilitude* (the appearance of seeming **real**), and *Veritaserum* (**truth** serum in the *Harry Potter* books and movies).

Vichyssoise means *a chilled soup of potatoes, leeks, and cream.* V is referring figuratively to a **soup** of words.

Verbiage means *long-winded speaking or writing.* Synonyms: circumlocution, loquacity, periphrasis, prolixity, superfluity, verbosity, wordiness.

Veers means *turns suddenly.*

Verbose means *long-winded.* For synonyms, let's turn to John Cusack's character, Vince Larkin, in *Con Air,* when he says, "That would be *loquacious, verbose, effusive . . .* how about *chatty?*" You can also add *garrulous, pleonastic, prolix,* and *voluble.*

Group 43

Here are two excerpts from a movie. See if you can name the movie, describe the scenes, and define the boldface vocabulary words. Check your answers on the following page.

SOPHIE: OK, what if one of your heroes came up to you and said . . . "Alex Fletcher, you are a horrible songwriter"? How would you react? . . .

ALEX: I would be horribly depressed. Yes, I would. But, then after months of brooding, I would find a lyricist and write a song about how horribly depressed I was, and it would be a big hit, and everyone would love me, and I'd make lots of money, and suddenly I'd be a lot less depressed than if I just sat around being a *little* bit self-indulgent and letting my misery eat away at me until I'd become an emotional wreck and creatively completely **moribund.** (*Sophie smiles, amused by his impressive word choice.*) Yes, moribund.

———

ALEX: I'll tell you what, look, we'll change your line about "places in my mind," if I can keep the chord sequence into the bridge, yeah?

SOPHIE: This isn't a negotiation. It's either right or wrong, inspired or **insipid.**

Movie: _____

Scenes: _____

_____

Moribund might mean _____

_____

Insipid might mean _____

_____

Hint: **SOPHIE:** That's wonderfully sensitive, Alex, especially from a man that wears such tight pants.
ALEX: It forces all the blood to my heart.

Solutions

Let's see how you did. Check your answers and write the exact definitions. To help you memorize the vocabulary words, reread the movie excerpts or even act out the scenes with a friend.

Movie: *Music and Lyrics,* Warner Bros. Pictures, 2007

Scenes: In the first excerpt, Sophie (Drew Barrymore) tells Alex (Hugh Grant) about her *debacle* (disaster) with Sloan Cates (Campbell Scott). She and Sloan had been dating until she discovered that he was engaged to someone else. After they broke up, he wrote a very insulting and very popular book, in which he criticized her writing style. In the second excerpt, Sophie and Alex are working on the song they are writing for reigning pop superstar, Cora (Haley Bennett).

Inside Scoop: You might recognize Matthew Morrison, who plays Cora's manager, Ray, from the Fox television show *Glee,* where he portrays Spanish teacher and Glee Club director, Will Schuester!

Moribund means *lacking vitality* or *dying. Moribund* comes from the root word *mort-* meaning *death,* as in *mortal* (*able to **die,*** as opposed to *immortal,* meaning *unable to die*) and *morbid* (gruesome).

Insipid means *flavorless, dull, and uninteresting.* Synonyms: banal, hackneyed, inane, jejune, lackluster, pedestrian, prosaic, trite, vacuous, vapid.

Group 44

Here's an excerpt from a movie. See if you can name the movie, describe the scene, and define the boldface vocabulary words. Check your answers on the following page.

PRINCE CHARMING: What? Where is he, Mum? (*draws his sword*) I shall **rend** his head from his shoulders! I will **smite** him where he stands! He will **rue** the very day he stole my kingdom from me! (*A bird poops on him.*)

FAIRY GODMOTHER: Oh, put it away, Junior! You're still gonna be king.

Movie: _____

Scene: _____

_____

Rend might mean _____

_____

Smite might mean _____

_____

Rue might mean _____

_____

Hint: "It was he who would chance the **perilous** journey through blistering cold and scorching desert, traveling for many days and nights, risking life and limb to reach the dragon's keep. For he was the bravest and most handsome in all the land, and it was destiny that his kiss would break the dreaded curse. He alone would climb to the highest room of the tallest tower to enter the princess's chambers, cross the room to her sleeping silhouette, pull back the **gossamer** curtains . . . " (*instead of a princess, he finds a wolf reading a magazine*)

Solutions

Let's see how you did. Check your answers and write the exact definitions. To help you memorize the vocabulary words, reread the movie excerpt or even act out the scene with a friend.

Movie: *Shrek 2,* DreamWorks, 2004

Scene: Fairy Godmother (voiced by Jennifer Saunders) tells Prince Charming (voiced by Rupert Everett) that Shrek (voiced by Mike Myers) broke into the potion factory and stole a "Happily Ever After" potion, which makes Prince Charming very upset.

Vocabulary in the Hint: *Perilous* means *dangerous. Gossamer* can refer to *the thin and very **delicate** cobwebs spun by small spiders* or to any substance that is *very thin and **delicate,*** like lace. For example, Stephenie Meyer uses this word quite often in the *Twilight* saga, such as to describe the beautiful, **delicate** white ribbons that decorate the Cullen's house for the party at the beginning of *Breaking Dawn.* Synonyms: diaphanous, sheer, wispy.

Rend means *tear apart.* Synonyms: sever, sunder, wrench. In fantasy role-playing games, *sunder* is an ability that allows a player to **slice an opponent's sword in two.** Now that vampires (think Edward Cullen), werewolves (can anyone say Team Jacob?), and even ogres (Shrek) are cool, you can't still be afraid of a little Dungeons & Dragons!

Smite means *strike heavily* or *defeat.*

Rue means *regret.* Synonyms for *rueful:* contrite, penitent, remorseful, repentant.

Group 45

Here are two excerpts from a movie. See if you can name the movie, describe the scenes, and define the boldface vocabulary words. Check your answers on the following page.

LINDA: Hi, I'm your **bereavement liaison**, Linda. My **consolations** for your loss.

FRANK: You know Marcel Proust?

DWAYNE: He's the guy you teach.

FRANK: Yeah. French writer. *Total* loser. Never had a real job. **Unrequited** love affairs . . . Spent twenty years writing a book almost no one reads. But he's also probably the greatest writer since Shakespeare. Anyway, he uh, he gets down to the end of his life, and he looks back and decides that all those years he suffered . . . those were the best years of his life, 'cause they made him who he was. All the years he was happy? You know, total waste. Didn't learn a thing. So, if you sleep until you're eighteen, ahh, think of the suffering you're gonna miss. I mean, high school? High school, those are your prime suffering years. You don't get better suffering than that.

Movie: _____

Scenes: _____

_____

Bereavement might mean _____

Liaison might mean _____

Consolations might mean _____

Unrequited might mean _____

Hint: The poster for this film shows the family running to get into their yellow Volkswagen T2 Microbus.

Solutions

Let's see how you did. Check your answers and write the exact definitions. To help you memorize the vocabulary words, reread the movie excerpts or even act out the scenes with a friend.

Movie: *Little Miss Sunshine,* Fox Searchlight Pictures, 2006

Scenes: In the first excerpt, Linda, a hospital grief counselor, is attending to the Hoover family after Grandpa (Alan Arkin) dies. In the second excerpt, Uncle Frank (Steve Carell) gives his nephew, Dwayne (Paul Dano), some advice. I love how this movie captures the angst and the joy of family, as well as the embarrassment and yet exhilaration of having to jump-start your family's beaten-up VW bus.

Bereavement means *grief from the loss of a loved one.*

Liaison means *agent* or *representative. Liaison* can also mean *secret love affair.*

Consolations means *sympathy* or *comfort.* Synonyms: condolences, solace.

Unrequited means *not returned.* Synonym: unreciprocated.

Group 46

Here's an excerpt from a movie. See if you can name the movie, describe the scene, and define the boldface vocabulary words. Check your answers on the following page.

SELENE: The Lycan **horde** scattered to the wind in a single evening of flame and **retribution.** Victory, it seemed, was in our grasp, the very birthright of the vampires. Nearly six centuries had passed since that night, yet the ancient blood feud proved unwilling to follow Lucian to the grave. Though Lycans were fewer in number, the war itself had become more **perilous,** for the moon no longer held her sway. Older, more powerful Lycans were now able to change at will. The weapons had evolved, but our orders remained the same: Hunt them down and kill them off, one by one. A most successful campaign. Perhaps too successful. For those like me, a Death Dealer, this signaled the end of an **era.** Like the weapons of the previous century, we, too, would become **obsolete.** Pity, because I lived for it.

Movie: _____

Scene: _____

_____

Horde might mean _____

Retribution might mean _____

Perilous might mean _____

Era might mean _____

Obsolete might mean _____

Hint: A vampire film without Robert Pattinson as Edward Cullen. Can it be true? In fact, in this vampire flick, the werewolf gets the girl!

Solutions

Let's see how you did. Check your answers and write the exact definitions. To help you memorize the vocabulary words, reread the movie excerpt or even act out the scene with a friend.

Movie: *Underworld,* Lakeshore Entertainment, 2003

Scene: *Underworld* describes a struggle between vampires and a type of werewolves that are called Lycans. Selene (Kate Beckinsale), a werewolf hunter, narrates at the beginning of the film just before she jumps down from a building to chase a werewolf.

Inside Scoop: In *Underworld,* werewolves are called *Lycans* (an abbreviation for *lycanthrope*). *Lyc-* refers to *wolf* and *anthro-* means *human,* so *lycanthrope* means *wolf-human.* Jacob Black of the *Twilight* saga would be right at home with these folks (although it turns out Jake's a shape-shifter, not a true werewolf).

Horde means *mob*. It can also refer to a *tribe of nomadic (traveling) warriors.* Synonym: throng.

Retribution means *revenge* or *punishment.* Synonyms: reprisal, requital, retaliation, retribution, vengeance.

Perilous means *dangerous.*

Era means *time period of history.* Synonyms: eon, epoch.

Obsolete means *outdated.* Synonyms: anachronistic, antediluvian, antiquated, archaic, bygone, defunct, démodé, extinct, outmoded, passé, superseded.

Here's an excerpt from a movie. See if you can name the movie, describe the scene, and define the boldface vocabulary words. Check your answers on the following page.

Doctor: His skin has lost all **elasticity,** and his hands and feet are **ossified.** He shows all the deterioration and the **infirmities** not of a newborn, but of a man well in his eighties on his way to the grave.

Movie: _____

Scene: _____

_____

Elasticity might mean _____

_____

Ossified might mean _____

_____

Infirmities might mean _____

_____

Hint: "For what it's worth, it's never too late, or in my case, too early, to be whoever you want to be. There's no time limit; start whenever you want . . . . I hope you live a life you're proud of. And, if you find that you're not, I hope you have the strength to start all over again."

Solutions

Let's see how you did. Check your answers and write the exact definitions. To help you memorize the vocabulary words, reread the movie excerpt or even act out the scene with a friend.

Movie: *The Curious Case of Benjamin Button,* Paramount Pictures, 2008

Scene: After Benjamin Button's (Brad Pitt) father leaves him on the steps of a nursing home, Queenie (Taraji P. Henson), a woman who works at the home, finds him. Regardless of the doctor's grim *prognosis* (diagnosis) of the baby's health, Queenie loves Benjamin wholeheartedly and gives him a home.

Inside Scoop: Brad Pitt and Angelina Jolie's own daughter, Shiloh Jolie-Pitt, plays one of the infants in the film.

Elasticity means *springiness,* like an elastic band being stretched and then **springing** back to its original position. The doctor means that Benjamin's skin is saggy and does not **spring** back into position if stretched. Synonyms: pliability, resilience, suppleness.

Ossified means *hardened* and comes from the root *oss-* meaning *bone,* which is very hard. *Ossified* can also mean *rigid and resistant to change,* which is the meaning usually used when this word appears on standardized tests. You can see the connection between the two meanings, when something is **hardened** it becomes more **resistant to change.**

Infirmities means *ailments* or *weaknesses.* Since *in-* means *not, infirm* literally means *not firm—ailing, weak.*

Group 48

Here are two excerpts from a movie. See if you can name the movie, describe the scenes, and define the boldface vocabulary words. Check your answers on the following page.

RECEPTIONIST: As we speak, interviews are being held at *Successful Saving*.

REBECCA: (*wearing a beautiful green scarf that she purchased for her interview at* Alette *magazine*) The money magazine?

RECEPTIONIST: Snort not, sweet child. *Alette* may be your emerald city, but *Successful Saving* could be your yellow brick road. Dante West is a family of magazines that acts like a family, deeply **nepotistic.** So my advice to you, dear Dorothy, is thus: once you're in, you're in.

_____

LUKE: A lot of people are very excited to meet you. You've opened up a whole new **demographic.**

Movie: _____

Scenes_____

_____

Nepotistic might mean _____

_____

Demographic might mean _____

_____

Hint: One of the movie poster taglines for this film was "A new job? Hopefully. A new man? Possibly. A new handbag? Absolutely!"

Solutions

Let's see how you did. Check your answers and write the exact definitions. To help you memorize the vocabulary words, reread the movie excerpts or even act out the scenes with a friend.

Movie: *Confessions of a Shopaholic,* Touchstone Pictures, 2009

Scenes: In the first excerpt, Rebecca (Isla Fisher) is at a magazine publisher's headquarters to interview for a job at *Alette* magazine, a fashion mag. She finds out the position has already been filled, but a helpful receptionist gives her a tip for a new way into the magazine. In the second excerpt, Rebecca's new boss, Luke (Hugh Dancy), invites her to a conference in Miami, and you see the first *overt* (obvious) romantic chemistry between the two.

Inside Scoop: Did you recognize *The Hangover*'s Ed Helms (Stu) as hilarious motivational speaker Garret E. Barton on Rebecca's DVD, *Control Your Urge to Shop?*

Nepotistic means *showing favoritism based on kinship or friendship.* The word derives from the Italian word for *nephew* and was used to describe an old practice whereby popes gave special privileges to their nephews, whom many believed were actually their illegitimate sons. That reminds me of the high-level SAT word *avuncular,* which means *of an uncle.* When you say it out loud, *avuncular* actually sounds like "of uncle"!

Demographic means *population of people.* Rebecca's "The Girl in the Green Scarf" magazine column has opened up a new **population of people** that read the magazine. *Demo-* means *people,* as in *democracy,* which means *government by the **people,*** since *-cracy* means *government.*

Group 49

Here are three excerpts from a movie. See if you can name the movie, describe the scenes, and define the boldface vocabulary words. Check your answers on the following page.

MIA: I'm sorry, OK? I forgot to call you and tell you that I couldn't make it.

LILLY: So I was stuck with the happy Houdini while you're making out with the yachting yahoo!

MIA: Those are really good **alliterations.**

_____

LILLY: Wanting to rock the world, but having zip power, like me, now that's a nightmare. But, you, wow!

MIA: OK, what is so "wow"?

LILLY: "Wow" is having the power to **effect** change, make people listen.

_____

QUEEN: I also came to apologize for the way I spoke to you about the beach incident. It was judgmental of me. I didn't pause to **verify** the facts.

Movie: _____

Scenes: _____

_____

Alliterations might mean _____

Effect might mean _____

Verify might mean _____

Hint: "And indeed, it is the queen of hearts! Thank you, Jeremiah, for your potpourri of **prestidigitation** for the past hour. Obviously, Princess Mia has a problem appearing here tonight, and I'm sure she has a good excuse."

Solutions

Let's see how you did. Check your answers and write the exact definitions. To help you memorize the vocabulary words, reread the movie excerpts or even act out the scenes with a friend.

Movie: *The Princess Diaries,* Walt Disney Pictures, 2001

Scenes: In the first excerpt, Mia (Anne Hathaway) apologizes to her friend, Lilly (Heather Matarazzo), for not showing up for her scheduled interview on Lilly's radio show. In the second excerpt, Lilly tries to convince Mia that being a princess would allow her to *effect* (bring about) change, and in the third excerpt, Mia's grandmother, the Queen of Genovia (Julie Andrews), apologizes to Mia for overreacting after the press photographed Mia with a boy at the beach.

Inside Scoop: For the scene in which Mia is wearing a dental retainer, Anne Hathaway brought in her old retainer.

Vocabulary in the Hint: *Prestidigitation* means *magic tricks. Prestidigitation* comes from *preste,* which is the French word for *nimble,* and *digitus,* which is the Latin word for *finger,* so *nimble fingers.* That's why a synonym for *prestidigitation* is *sleight of hand.*

Alliterations refers to *the literary device of using the same consonant sound at the beginning of successive words,* such as "happy Houdini" or "yachting yahoo." If you take the SAT Subject Test in Literature, you are likely to see this word on the test.

Effect in this case means *bring about.* The verb *effect* means *bring about,* whereas the verb *affect* means *influence* or *have an effect on,* such as "studying more will **affect** your grades."

Verify means *confirm. Veri-* refers to *truth,* so *verify* means *confirm the **truth** of. Veri-* makes me think of *Veritaserum* (from the *Harry Potter* books), which forces the drinker to speak only the **truth,** and it can also help you remember high-level SAT words like *verity* (a fundamental **truth**), *veracity* (**truthfulness**), and *verisimilitude* (the appearance of seeming real or **true**).

Group 50

Here's an excerpt from a movie. See if you can name the movie, describe the scene, and define the boldface vocabulary words. Check your answers on the following page.

DEAN KANSKY: Kids your age, pimple-faced college drop-outs who have made unhealthy sums of money forming Internet companies that create no concrete products, provide no **viable** services, and still manage to generate profits for all of its lazy, day trading, son-of-a-bitch shareholders. Meanwhile, as a tortured member of the **disenfranchised proletariat**, you find some **altruistic** need to protect these digital plantation owners?

Movie: _____

Scene: _____

_____

Viable might mean _____

_____

Disenfranchised might mean _____

_____

Proletariat might mean _____

_____

Altruistic might mean _____

_____

Hint: JONATHAN: Where'd you find this place?
SARA: I first came in because of the name: **Serendipity.** It's one of my favorite words.
JONATHAN: It is? Why?
SARA: It's just such a nice sound for what it means: *a fortunate accident.*

Solutions

Let's see how you did. Check your answers and write the exact definitions. To help you memorize the vocabulary words, reread the movie excerpt or even act out the scene with a friend.

Movie: *Serendipity*, Miramax Films, 2001

Scene: This excerpt was delivered in the film by Dean Kansky, played by Jeremy Piven in a wonderfully Ari Gold–esque *diatribe* (angry, attacking speech); this film was shot three years before the HBO series *Entourage*, but Ari's character must have already been brewing in Piven's mind. In the excerpt, Dean and Jonathan (John Cusack) are trying to convince a low-level office worker to release confidential information about a client. The information would help them track down Jonathan's lost love, Sara Thomas (Kate Beckinsale).

Inside Scoop: This film sports an amazing cast including John Cusack, Kate Beckinsale, Molly Shannon, Jeremy Piven (Ari on *Entourage*), John Corbett (Aidan on *Sex and the City*), and Eugene Levy (Jim's dad in *American Pie*).

Vocabulary in the Hint: *Serendipity*, as Sara says, means *a fortunate accident*.

Viable means *possible*. Synonym: feasible.

Disenfranchised means *disempowered*. *Dis-* basically means *not*, and *franchised* means *empowered* or *licensed*, or more specifically *given the right to vote*. That's why individual McDonald's restaurants are called *franchises*—they have been given **licenses** and are **empowered** by the McDonald's Corporation to do business as a McDonald's.

Proletariat means *working class*. Synonyms: hoi polloi, plebeians. Antonym: aristocracy (the upper class or nobility).

Altruistic means *selfless*. Synonyms: beneficent, benevolent, bounteous, charitable, humanitarian, munificent, philanthropic.

Quiz 5

I. Let's review some of the words that you've seen in Groups 41–50.
Match each of the following words to the correct definition or synonym
on the right. If you need help, refer back to the movie excerpts and definitions. Then check the solutions on page 237.

1. Petulant	A. Opportune
2. Proximity	B. Lacking vitality
3. Auspicious	C. Peevish
4. Verbiage	D. Solace
5. Moribund	E. Sunder
6. Insipid	F. Propinquity
7. Rend	G. Verbosity
8. Rueful	H. Vacuous
9. Unrequited	I. Hardened
10. Consolation	J. Contrite
11. Horde	K. Unreciprocated
12. Obsolete	L. Munificent
13. Ossified	M Defunct
14. Verify	N. Throng
15. Altruistic	O. Confirm

II. Let's review several of the word parts that you've seen in Groups
41–50. Match each of the following word parts to the correct definition or
synonym on the right. Then check the solutions on page 237.

16. Dis- (as in *disenfranchised*)	A. Death
17. Anthro- (as in *anthropomorphism*)	B. Bone
	C. Humans
18. Veri- (as in *verify*)	D. Not
19. Mort- (as in *mortal*)	E. Truth
20. Oss- (as in *ossified*)	

III. Match each group of synonyms to its general meaning. Then check the solutions on page 237.

21. Cantankerous
    Churlish
    Curmudgeonly
    Fractious
    Irascible
    Peevish
    Petulant
    Querulous
    Sullen

      A. Wordy

22. Auspicious
    Felicitous
    Opportune
    Propitious
    Providential

      B. Regretful

23. Effusive
    Garrulous
    Loquacious
    Pleonastic
    Prolix
    Verbose
    Voluble

      C. Irritable

24. Contrite
    Penitent
    Remorseful
    Repentant
    Rueful

      D. Selfless

25. Altruistic
    Beneficent
    Bounteous
    Charitable
    Munificent

      E. Fortunate

Group 51

Here are two excerpts from a movie. See if you can name the movie, describe the scenes, and define the boldface vocabulary words. Check your answers on the following page.

WILL: (*to Emily*) It's two months in New York; I'll be back before you know it . . .

CHARLIE: (*to Will*) One thing I can't believe is that you'd risk leaving Emily here with me, because I've got to tell you, I've always had a thing for you, Em. (*Will throws a bike helmet at Charlie.*) And I have absolutely no **scruples.**

_____

WILL: You take the simplest statement and then you twist it with a completely negative **connotation.** It's really actually impressive . . . It's probably hard for you to imagine a relationship based on mutual respect without even the slightest hint of, whatever you call it, **masochism** . . .

APRIL: Why do you want to marry me besides some **bourgeois** desire to fulfill an ideal that society **embeds** in us from an early age to promote a consumer **capitalist** agenda?

Movie: _____

Scenes: _____

Scruples might mean _____

Connotation might mean _____

Masochism might mean _____

Bourgeois might mean _____

Embeds might mean _____

Capitalist might mean _____

Hint: "Will you, um, marry me?"

Solutions

Let's see how you did. Check your answers and write the exact definitions. To help you memorize the vocabulary words, reread the movie excerpts or even act out the scenes with a friend.

Movie: *Definitely, Maybe,* Universal Pictures, 2008

Scenes: In the first excerpt, Will (Ryan Reynolds) is leaving Wisconsin and his college sweetheart, Emily (Elizabeth Banks), for a job in New York City where he will work on Bill Clinton's election campaign. In the second excerpt, Will is at a party with April (Isla Fisher), a woman who is also working on the campaign.

Scruples means *concerns about being immoral.* Synonyms: compunctions, qualms.

Connotation means *implication.*

Masochism means *the practice of seeking pain.* The opposite of a *masochist* is a *sadist* (one who likes to **inflict** rather than **experience** pain). The word *sadist* actually comes from the name of the Marquis de **Sade**, who is known for some pretty freaky and disturbing activities. The Marquis was the subject of the movie *Quills* (from 2000), costarring Geoffrey Rush and Kate Winslet.

Bourgeois means *the conventional and materialistic middle class.* This reminds me of the word *proletariat* (working class) from the *Serendipity* scene in Group 50. Synonym: provincial.

Embeds means *puts firmly in place.*

Capitalist means *relating to the profit-based economic system in which resources are privately owned.*

Group 52

Here are two excerpts from a movie. See if you can name the movie, describe the scenes, and define the boldface vocabulary words. Check your answers on the following page.

MRS. AUSTEN: Jane does enjoy a ball!

LADY GRESHAM: Wisley can't **abide** them.

JANE: (*to Wisley*) But, Sir, a ball is an **indispensable** blessing to the **juvenile** part of the neighborhood. Everything agreeable in the way of talking and sitting down together, all managed with the utmost **decorum.** An **amiable** man could not object.

_____

JANE: (*to Tom Lefroy*) This, by the way, is called a country dance, after the French, *contredanse*. Not because it is exhibited at an uncouth **rural** assembly with glutinous pies, **execrable** Madeira, and truly **anarchic** dancing.

Movie: _____

Scenes: _____

Abide might mean _____

Indispensable might mean _____

Juvenile might mean _____

Decorum might mean _____

Amiable might mean _____

Rural might mean _____

Execrable might mean _____

Anarchic might mean _____

Hint: Anne Hathaway and James McAvoy

Solutions

Let's see how you did. Check your answers and write the exact definitions. To help you memorize the vocabulary words, reread the movie excerpts or even act out the scenes with a friend.

Movie: *Becoming Jane,* Miramax Films, 2007

Scenes: In the first excerpt, Jane Austen's mother (Julie Walters) tries to set her up with a potential suitor, Mr. Wisley (Laurence Fox), nephew of the wealthy Lady Gresham (Maggie Smith). In the second excerpt, Jane (Anne Hathaway) is dancing and flirting with her brother's friend, Tom Lefroy (James McAvoy), who has a bad reputation.

Abide means *tolerate* or *obey*.

Indispensable means *essential*. Synonyms: imperative, invaluable, requisite, vital. Antonym: superfluous (unnecessary).

Juvenile means *childish or immature*. Synonyms: puerile, sophomoric.

Decorum means *proper behavior*. Synonyms: conventions, etiquette, propriety, protocol, punctilio. *Star Wars'* C-3PO is a **protocol** droid (human-like robot), meaning he helps his owner with the **rules of proper behavior** when interacting with other cultures.

Amiable means *friendly and pleasant* and comes from *amicus-,* which means *friend,* like *amigo* in Spanish, or *ami* in French. Synonyms: affable, amicable, convivial, cordial, genial, gregarious, simpatico.

Rural means *of the countryside, rather than the city*. Synonyms: bucolic, pastoral, rustic. Antonym: urban.

Execrable means *appalling*. Synonyms: abhorrent, abysmal, atrocious, deplorable, egregious, lamentable, loathsome, odious, reprehensible, vile.

Anarchic means *without order*. Synonym: chaotic.

Group 53

Here are two excerpts from a movie. See if you can name the movie, describe the scenes, and define the boldface vocabulary words. Check your answers on the following page.

R.H.: The entire family will be **implicated** if this ends badly.

B.S.: Badly as in . . . I would become the meal.

_____

B.S.: Graduation caps?

E.C.: Ah, yeah. It's a private joke. We **matriculate** a lot.

Movie: _____

Scenes: _____

_____

Implicated might mean _____

_____

Matriculate might mean _____

_____

Hint: E.C.: And so the lion fell in love with the lamb.
   B.S.: What a stupid lamb.
   E.C.: What a sick, **masochistic** lion.

Solutions

Let's see how you did. Check your answers and write the exact definitions. To help you memorize the vocabulary words, reread the movie excerpts or even act out the scenes with a friend.

Movie: *Twilight,* Summit Entertainment, 2008

Scenes: Sorry for using Bella, Edward, and Rosalie's initials, but saying "Bella Swan," "Edward Cullen," or even "Rosalie Hale" might have given it away about as much as writing "Captain Jack Sparrow" for a *Pirates of the Caribbean* excerpt.

Inside Scoop: Robert Pattinson auditioned for the role of Edward Cullen at the home of director Catherine Hardwicke—he and Kristen Stewart, who was already cast as Bella Swan, performed the Meadow Scene right on Hardwicke's own bed!

Vocabulary in the Hint: *Masochistic* means *liking and seeking pain*. In this famous quote from *Twilight,* Edward is referring to himself as a lion, and Bella as the lamb. The Lion is **masochistic** because it would be **painful** to be in love with someone who you also want to kill.

Implicated means *involved, held responsible,* or *implied*. Synonyms: compromised, embroiled, enmeshed, ensnared, entangled, incriminated.

Matriculate means *enroll in school*. The Cullens enroll in school a lot (each time they move to a new town and pretend to be high-school students) and that's why the mural of graduation caps on the wall is a "private joke."

Group 54

Here are two excerpts from a movie. See if you can name the movie, describe the scenes, and define the boldface vocabulary words. Check your answers on the following page.

Mom: Beautiful gowns for my darling **debutante**.

Viola: Mom, have I not told you a thousand times? I have no interest in being a debutante. It's totally **archaic**.

Mom: How could I wind up with a daughter who only wants to kick a muddy ball around a field all day?

———————

Viola: Euni . . . (*clears throat to deepen voice*) Eunice, why didn't you wake me?!

Eunice: You looked so **serene**.

Movie: _____

Scenes: _____

_____

Debutante might mean _____

_____

Archaic might mean _____

_____

Serene might mean _____

_____

Hint: "Just so you know, everything you told me when I was a guy just made me like you so much more as a girl."

Solutions

Let's see how you did. Check your answers and write the exact definitions. To help you memorize the vocabulary words, reread the movie excerpts or even act out the scenes with a friend.

Movie: *She's the Man*, DreamWorks, 2006

Scenes: In the first excerpt, Viola's mom shows Viola (Amanda Bynes) potential gowns for the debutante ball, and in the second excerpt, Viola stayed the night in Eunice's (Emily Perkins) room and has woken up late for the big soccer game. Viola is pretending to be her twin brother in order to play on the boys' soccer team. She clears her throat to deepen her voice, so that Eunice will continue to believe that she is a guy.

Inside Scoop: *She's the Man* is based on Shakespeare's *Twelfth Night*. Channing Tatum, in his first major film role, plays Viola's love interest, Duke.

Debutante looks like *debut* (first appearance) and refers to *a young woman making her official first appearance as a woman in high society*.

Archaic means *outdated* and was a synonym for *obsolete* on the *Underworld* page (Group 46). Synonyms: anachronistic, antediluvian, antiquated, bygone, defunct, démodé, extinct, obsolete, outmoded, passé.

Serene means *calm and peaceful*. Synonyms: equanimous, placid, poised (calm and composed), tranquil.

Group 55

Here's an excerpt from a movie. See if you can name the movie, describe the scene, and define the boldface vocabulary words. Check your answers on the following page.

ALEX: I put up pretty **pedestrian** numbers, like 60,000 a year domestic.

RYAN: That's not bad.

ALEX: Don't **patronize** me. What's your total?

RYAN: That's a personal question.

ALEX: Oh, please.

RYAN: We hardly know each other.

ALEX: Oh, come on, show some **hubris.** Come on, impress me.

Movie: _____

Scene: _____

_____

Pedestrian might mean _____

_____

Patronize might mean _____

_____

Hubris might mean _____

_____

Hint: "What's in your backpack? . . . Some animals were meant to carry each other, to live **symbiotically** over a lifetime: **star-crossed** lovers, **monogamous** swans. We are not swans. We're sharks."

Solutions

Let's see how you did. Check your answers and write the exact definitions. To help you memorize the vocabulary words, reread the movie excerpt or even act out the scene with a friend.

Movie: *Up in the Air,* Paramount Pictures, 2009

Scene: Ryan (George Clooney) sees Alex (Vera Farmiga) in a hotel bar and strikes up a conversation. Both are frequent business travelers, and they get turned on comparing their premier frequent-flyer and hotel-club cards.

Inside Scoop: Did you recognize Anna Kendrick (*Twilight*'s Jessica Stanley) as Natalie?

Vocabulary in the Hint: *Symbiotically* means *mutually beneficially.* *Monogamous* means *committed to one sexual partner.* *Star-crossed* means *doomed.* This is an excerpt from Ryan's "What's in Your Backpack?" motivational speech.

Pedestrian can mean *ordinary and unimaginative.* Of course, *pedestrian* can also refer to *someone walking.* Synonyms: conventional, prosaic. *Prosaic* comes from the word *prose,* which refers to *ordinary writing,* as opposed to *poetry,* which has a less **ordinary** structure and is often more **imaginative.**

Patronize in this case means *treat kindly, but with a superior attitude.* It can also mean *supporting* or *being a customer,* like shopping at a store or eating at a restaurant. Standardized tests love words with multiple meanings. On a reading comprehension question, make sure to check the word's use in the passage to see which meaning is appropriate. Synonyms: condescend, demean, denigrate. *Patronizing* reminds me of the word *supercilious* (acting superior, arrogant), which was a synonym for *haughty* in the *Bridget Jones* excerpt (Group 5).

Hubris means *pride.* Synonyms: arrogance, conceit, haughtiness, hauteur, egotism, pomposity, superciliousness. Antonym: humility.

Group 56

Here are two excerpts from a movie. See if you can name the movie, describe the scenes, and define the boldface vocabulary words. Check your answers on the following page.

NOAH: I can be fun, if you want, . . . **pensive,** . . . uh, smart, uh, **superstitious,** brave. And, uh, I can be light on my feet. (*does a little dance*) I could be whatever you want. You just tell me what you want, and I'll be that for you.

ALLIE: You're dumb.

NOAH: I could be that. (*smiles*) Come on, one date. What's it gonna hurt?

NARRATOR: Summer romances end for all kinds of reasons. But when all is said and done, they have one thing in common: They are shooting stars, a spectacular moment of light in the heavens, a **fleeting** glimpse of **eternity**. And in a flash, they're gone. Noah was **desperate.** He wrote to Allie that he was sorry and stupid for breaking up with her.

Movie: _____

Scenes: _____

_____

Pensive might mean _____

Superstitious might mean _____

Fleeting might mean _____

Eternity might mean _____

Desperate might mean _____

Hint: "*The Story of Our Lives,* by Allie Calhoun. Read this to me, and I'll come back to you."

Solutions

Let's see how you did. Check your answers and write the exact definitions. To help you memorize the vocabulary words, reread the movie excerpts or even act out the scenes with a friend.

Movie: *The Notebook,* New Line Cinema, 2004

Scenes: In the first excerpt, Noah (Ryan Gosling) sees Allie (Rachel McAdams) walking on the street and goes over to ask her out. This is the scene after he had jumped onto the Ferris wheel and made her promise to go out with him. In the second excerpt, Noah and Allie have broken up, and her family has moved her away to separate them.

Inside Scoop: I love seeing a young Kevin Connolly (Eric from HBO's *Entourage*) in this movie as Noah's best friend, Fin!

Pensive means *introspective.* If you're a *Wedding Crashers* fan, you might remember this word from *Wedding Crashers* Rule #50: "Be Pensive! It draws out the healer in women." You might also remember Dumbledore's Pensieve, in the *Harry Potter* books and movies, which he uses to see **thoughts** and memories. Synonyms: brooding, contemplative, meditative, musing, reflective, ruminative.

Superstitious means *believing in supernatural causes and effects,* such as seven years of bad luck from breaking a mirror.

Fleeting means *disappearing or passing quickly.* Synonyms: ephemeral, evanescent, fugitive, impermanent, transient, transitory.

Eternity means *timelessness* or *forever.*

Desperate means *miserable, extremely needy,* or *hopeless.* Synonyms: anguished, desolate, despairing, despondent, distraught, forlorn, wretched.

Group 57

Here are two excerpts from a movie. See if you can name the movie, describe the scenes, and define the boldface vocabulary words. Check your answers on the following page.

DARCY: (*at tryouts*) Bring on the **tyros,** the **neophytes,** and the **dilettantes.**

JAN: SATs are over, Darcy.

DARCY: And you're still jealous of my score. Are we sure Carver's not **malingering** . . .

———————

MISSY: (*While washing cars and wearing a bikini at a cheerleading team fundraiser, Missy greets her brother.*) Hey, perve. Hand over your fifteen bucks or get out of here.

CLIFF: What are you doing?

MISSY: Making money from guys **ogling** my goodies.

CLIFF: Ahh, I didn't need to hear that. That was an over-share.

Movie: _____

Scenes: _____

Tyros might mean _____

Neophytes might mean _____

Dilettantes might mean _____

Malingering might mean _____

Ogling might mean _____

Hint: "What you do is a tiny, **pathetic** subset of dancing. I will attempt to transform your robotic routines into poetry, written with the human body. Follow me or **perish,** sweater monkeys."

Solutions

Let's see how you did. Check your answers and write the exact definitions. To help you memorize the vocabulary words, reread the movie excerpts or even act out the scenes with a friend.

Movie: *Bring It On,* Universal Studios, 2000

Scenes: In the first excerpt, the cheerleading squad at Rancho Carne High School is getting ready to audition applicants to fill Carver's position on the team—Carver got injured during practice. In the second excerpt, Missy (Eliza Dushku) greets her brother, Cliff (Jesse Bradford), at the cheerleading squad's carwash fundraiser. I love how Cliff delivers the hilarious line "That was an over-share."

Inside Scoop: Brandi Williams, Shamari Fears, and Natina Reed of the R&B trio *Blaque* play three of the East Compton High School cheerleaders. At one point in the movie, Jenelope (Natina Reed) refers to Torrance (Kirsten Dunst) and Missy as "Buffies." This is an inside joke because Eliza Dushku, who plays Missy, had been on the TV show *Buffy the Vampire Slayer.*

Vocabulary in the Hint: The psycho choreographer, Sparky Polast-sri, delivers this *diatribe* (angry, attacking speech). *Pathetic* means *pitiful. Perish* means *become ruined* or *die.*

Tyros means *beginners.* Darcy (Tsianina Joelson) expected only **beginners** at the tryouts. She did not expect anyone like Missy, gymnast extraordinaire, to show up. Torrance is impressed by Missy and tells Darcy, "Missy's the poo, so take a big whiff!" Synonyms: fledglings, initiates, neophytes, novices, probationers, tenderfoots. Antonym: veterans.

Neophytes means *beginners.* Synonyms: fledglings, initiates, novices, probationers, tenderfoots, tyros. Antonym: veterans.

Dilettantes means *amateurs* or *people who take part in something in a casual and uncommitted way.* Synonym: dabblers.

Malingering means *faking illness to avoid school or work.*

Ogling means *staring with excessive or offensive sexual desire.*

Here are a bunch of excerpts from a movie. See if you can name the movie, describe the scenes, and define the boldface vocabulary words. Check your answers on the following pages.

JACK: Tia Dalma, out and about, eh? You add an agreeable sense of the **macabre** to any **delirium.**

JACK: *"Captain* Turner"?

MR. GIBBS: Aye, the **perfidious** rotter led a mutiny against us.

JACK: You can keep Barbossa; the **belligerent homunculus** and his friend with the wooden eye, both; and Turner, especially Turner. The rest go with me aboard the *Pearl*. And I'll lead you to Shipwreck Cove.

BARBOSSA: Calypso! I come before you as but a servant, humble and **contrite.** I have fulfilled me vow and now ask your favor.

JACK: Ladies, will you please shut it?! Listen to me. Yes, I lied to you. No, I don't love you. Of course it makes you look fat. I've never been to Brussels. It is pronounced *ih-gree-juhs.* By the way, no, I've never actually met Pizarro, but I love his pies. And all of this pales to utter insignificance in light of the fact that my ship is once again gone. Savvy?

Movie: _____

Scenes: _____

_____

Hint: "Wouldn't it be amazing if this venture of yours took you to the world beyond this one?"

Macabre might mean _____

_____

Delirium might mean _____

_____

Perfidious might mean _____

_____

Belligerent might mean _____

_____

Homumculus might mean _____

_____

Contrite might mean _____

_____

Egregious might mean _____

_____

Solutions

Let's see how you did. Check your answers and write the exact definitions. To help you memorize the vocabulary words, reread the movie excerpts or even act out the scenes with a friend.

Movie: *Pirates of the Caribbean: At World's End,* Walt Disney Pictures, 2007

Scenes: In the first excerpt, Jack (Johnny Depp), imprisoned in Davy Jones' locker, greets Tia Dalma (Naomie Harris) and the rest of his rescue party. In the second excerpt, he is surprised to hear Sao Feng (Chow Yun-fat), pirate lord of the South China Sea, refer to Will Turner (Orlando Bloom) as "Captain." In the third, Jack negotiates with Lord Cutler Beckett (Tom Hollander), of the East India Trading Company, who is attempting to execute anyone associated with piracy. In the fourth excerpt, Barbossa (Geoffrey Rush) frees the sea goddess Calypso (Naomie Harris), and in the fifth, Jack chats with two ladies in port. This movie contains a *profusion* (abundance) of vocabulary words and is a must-see before your next standardized test!

Macabre means *bloody, deathly,* or *gruesome.* Synonyms: ghastly, gory, morbid.

Delirium means *madness characterized by confused thinking, disrupted speech, and hallucinations.* Synonyms: dementia, derangement, hallucination, hysteria, incoherence.

Perfidious means *disloyal.* Synonyms: deceitful, duplicitous, traitorous, treacherous, treasonous.

Belligerent means *hostile.* Synonyms: bellicose, inimical, pugnacious, truculent.

Homunculus means *miniature humanoid.*

Contrite means *regretful for wrongdoing.* Synonyms: penitent, remorseful, repentant.

Egregious means *shocking* or *terribly bad.* Synonyms: abhorrent, abominable, appalling, atrocious, dreadful, grievous, heinous, horrendous. You can throw in Bart Simpson's invented word "craptastic" as a synonym as well.

Group 59

Here are three excerpts from a movie. See if you can name the movie, describe the scenes, and define the boldface vocabulary words. Check your answers on the following page.

KAREN EIFFEL: (*narrating*) Little did he know that this simple, seemingly **innocuous** act would result in his **imminent** death.

HAROLD CRICK: Dave, can I pose a somewhat **abstract,** purely **hypothetical** question?

DAVE: Sure.

HAROLD CRICK: If you knew you were going to die, possibly soon, what would you do?

HAROLD CRICK: What's this?

ANA PASCAL: My tax files.

HAROLD CRICK: You keep your files like this?

ANA PASCAL: No. Actually, I'm quite **fastidious.** I put them in this box just to screw with you.

Movie: _____

Scenes: _____

Innocuous might mean _____

Imminent might mean _____

Abstract might mean _____

Hypothetical might mean _____

Fastidious might mean _____

Hint: "I'm being followed by a woman's voice . . . She's narrating."

Solutions

Let's see how you did. Check your answers and write the exact definitions. To help you memorize the vocabulary words, reread the movie excerpts or even act out the scenes with a friend.

Movie: *Stranger than Fiction,* Columbia Pictures, 2006

Scenes: In the first excerpt, Karen Eiffel (Emma Thompson) is narrating Harold Crick's (Will Ferrell) life. In the second excerpt, Harold confides in an IRS coworker, and in the third excerpt, Harold *audits* (reviews) Ana's (Maggie Gyllenhaal) tax records because she paid only part of the taxes that she owes for her bakery.

Innocuous means *harmless.* Synonym: benign.

Imminent means *happening soon.* Synonyms: forthcoming, impending, looming.

Abstract means *theoretical rather than actual.*

Hypothetical means *theoretical.* Synonyms: conjectural, notional, putative, speculative, supposed, suppositional.

Fastidious means *very clean* or *very attentive to details.* Synonyms: assiduous, finicky, meticulous, punctilious, scrupulous, sedulous. Remember to say or write each boldface word and its list of synonyms five times. I've seen every one of the words in this list on standardized tests. Memorize them and your score will go up!

Group 60

Here's an excerpt from a movie. See if you can name the movie, describe the scene, and define the boldface vocabulary words. Check your answers on the following page.

ROMAN: Danny, I like you. And you, Rusty. I mean, you've got style. You've got **brio.** You've got loyalty . . . Believe me, I would love to go up against Greco and crush him, but it can't be beat. It can't be hacked, and it can't be beat.

DANNY: Not even by you?

ROMAN: Oh, with eighteen months, nothing else on my plate, no other jobs, no women, no distractions, maybe.

RUSTY: You know everything about this thing?

ROMAN: Everything except where it was being **deployed.** The inventor's an old schoolmate of mine. His name is Greco Montgomery. **Pompous** arse named it after himself . . . The Greco is housed in an **impregnable** room.

Movie: _____

Scene: _____

_____

Brio might mean _____

Deployed might mean _____

Pompous might mean _____

Impregnable might mean _____

Hint: Eleven, Twelve, Thirteen

Solutions

Let's see how you did. Check your answers and write the exact definitions. To help you memorize the vocabulary words, reread the movie excerpt or even act out the scene with a friend.

Movie: *Ocean's Thirteen,* Warner Bros., 2007

Scene: Danny Ocean (George Clooney) and Rusty (Brad Pitt) are looking for help from techie wizard Roman Nagel (Eddie Izzard) to hack the computer system, known as the Greco, at Willy Bank's (Al Pacino) new casino.

Brio means *spirit.* Synonyms: gusto, verve, vigor, vivacity, zest.

Deployed means *utilized* or *positioned.*

Pompous means *arrogant.* Synonyms: affected, conceited, egotistic, haughty, pontifical, pretentious, sententious, supercilious, uppity, vain.

Impregnable means *unable to be broken into.* Synonyms: impenetrable, inviolable, invulnerable, unassailable.

Quiz 6

I. Let's review some of the words that you've seen in Groups 51 –60. Match each of the following words to the correct definition or synonym on the right. If you need help, refer back to the movie excerpts and definitions. Then check the solutions on page 238.

1.	Bourgeois	A.	Propriety
2.	Juvenile	B.	Prosaic
3.	Decorum	C.	Sophomoric
4.	Amiable	D.	Ephemeral
5.	Serene	E.	Provincial
6.	Pedestrian	F.	Genial
7.	Hubris	G.	Duplicitous
8.	Fleeting	H.	Superciliousness
9.	Tyros	I.	Equanimous
10.	Macabre	J.	Truculent
11.	Perfidious	K.	Assiduous
12.	Belligerent	L.	Neophytes
13.	Contrite	M.	Penitent
14.	Innocuous	N.	Morbid
15.	Fastidious	O.	Benign

II. Let's review several of the word parts that you've seen in Groups 51–60. Match each of the following word parts to the correct definition or synonym on the right. Then check the solutions on page 238.

16.	Amicus- (as in *amicable*)	A.	Bone
	Review:	B.	Death
17.	Veri- (as in *verify*)	C.	One
18.	Mort- (as in *mortal*)	D.	Friend
19.	Oss- (as in *ossified*)	E.	Truth
20.	Mono- (as in *monarch*)		

III. Match each group of synonyms to its general meaning. Then check the solutions on page 238.

21. Conventional
    Pedestrian
    Prosaic

A. Pride

22. Haughtiness
    Hubris
    Pomposity
    Superciliousness

B. Disloyal

23. Ephemeral
    Evanescent
    Fleeting
    Transient

C. Ordinary and unimaginative

24. Duplicitous
    Perfidious
    Treacherous

D. Attentive to details

25. Bellicose
    Belligerent
    Inimical
    Pugnacious
    Truculent

E. Disappearing quickly

26. Assiduous
    Fastidious
    Meticulous
    Punctilious
    Scrupulous
    Sedulous

F. Hostile

Group 61

Here's an excerpt from a movie. See if you can name the movie, describe the scene, and define the boldface vocabulary words. Check your answers on the following page.

ALPHONSO: "The way of love is not a subtle argument. The door there is **devastation.**" (*holds up a book by Rumi*)

REED: So, according to Rumi, love has to be devastating?

ALPHONSO: Listen, you don't step into love, my friend, you fall in, head over heels. You ever seen somebody fall head over heels in love, for real, Reed? It's ugly, bro, toxic, **septic.** Come on, boss, you still got a few hours left. Make something happen . . .

REED: Hey, tell me something, how'd you and your wife get it so right?

ALPHONSO: That's easy. I married my best friend.

Movie: _____

Scene: _____

_____

Devastation might mean _____

_____

Septic might mean _____

_____

Hint: February 14

Solutions

Let's see how you did. Check your answers and write the exact definitions. To help you memorize the vocabulary words, reread the movie excerpt or even act out the scene with a friend.

Movie: *Valentine's Day,* Warner Bros., 2010

Scene: Alphonso (George Lopez) gives Reed (Ashton Kutcher) advice about love. The book that Alphonso is holding is *The Essential Rumi,* translated by Coleman Barks. Rumi was a thirteenth century Persian poet, theologian, and mystic who wrote love poems to God. His poems are considered among the finest in history.

Inside Scoop: This movie stars Julia Roberts, Bradley Cooper, Ashton Kutcher, Jessica Alba, Patrick Dempsey, Anne Hathaway, Jessica Biel, Jamie Foxx, Jennifer Garner, George Lopez, Hector Elizondo, Kathy Bates, Emma Roberts, Carter Jenkins, Bryce Robinson, Taylor Swift, Taylor Lautner, Eric Dane, Queen Latifah, Shirley MacLaine, and Topher Grace!

Devastation means *destruction* or *agony.* Synonyms: anguish, annihilation, demolition, desolation, despoliation, havoc, ruination, wreckage.

Septic means *infected.* You can see this word's relationship to a ***septic*** *tank* (a tank in which sewage is collected). Synonyms: festering, purulent, putrefying, putrid, suppurating.

Group 62

Here are two excerpts from a movie. See if you can name the movie, describe the scenes, and define the boldface vocabulary words. Check your answers on the following page.

BENDER: Hey, how come Andrew gets to get up? If he gets up, we'll all get up. It will be **anarchy!**

BENDER: *(after Claire gives him "the finger")* Oh, obscene finger gestures from such a **pristine** girl.

Movie: _____

Scenes: _____

_____

Anarchy might mean _____

_____

Pristine might mean _____

_____

Hint: "Dear Mr. Vernon, we accept the fact that we had to sacrifice a whole Saturday in detention for whatever it was we did wrong. What we did *was* wrong. But we think you're crazy to make us write an essay telling you who we think we are. What do you care? You see us as you want to see us. In the simplest terms, the most convenient definitions. You see us as a brain, an athlete, a basket case, a princess, and a criminal. Correct? That's the way we saw each other at seven o'clock this morning."

Solutions

Let's see how you did. Check your answers and write the exact definitions. To help you memorize the vocabulary words, reread the movie excerpts or even act out the scenes with a friend.

Movie: *The Breakfast Club,* Universal Studios, 1985

Scenes: In the first excerpt, Principal Vernon (Paul Gleason) has asked Andrew (Emilio Estevez) to get up from his seat in detention in order to help prop the door open. Bender (Judd Nelson), eager to cause trouble, makes a fuss. In the second excerpt, Claire (Molly Ringwald) gives Bender the finger after he taunts her. This movie is an absolute classic, a must-see for any high school student. Actually, you should see all of John Hughes' (the director) high school dramas: *The Breakfast Club, Ferris Bueller's Day Off, Pretty in Pink, Sixteen Candles, Some Kind of Wonderful,* and *Weird Science.*

Anarchy means *disorder*. Synonyms: bedlam, chaos, mayhem, pandemonium, turmoil. *An-* means *without* and *-archy* means *ruler,* so *anarchy* means *without ruler—the absence of law.* The suffix *-archy* helps you remember words like *monarchy* (*mono-* means *one,* so *monarchy* means *rule by one—* usually by a king or queen), *oligarchy* (*oligo-* means *a small number,* so *oligarchy* means *rule by a small group of individuals*), *matriarchy* (rule by women), and *plutarchy* (rule by the wealthy).

Pristine means *pure* or *perfect*. Synonyms: immaculate, intact.

Group 63

Here are three excerpts from a movie. See if you can name the movie, describe the scenes, and define the boldface vocabulary words. Check your answers on the following page.

JAMES: It's always the same **inane** questions, (*for example*) "Who are you?"

VICTORIA: (*another example*) "What do you want?"

JAMES: (*another example*) "Why are you doing this?"

LAURENT: James, let's not play with our food.

———————

E.C.: You don't know the **vile, repulsive** things they were thinking.

B.S.: And you do?

———————

E.C.: That's because you believe the lie, the **camouflage.** I'm the world's most dangerous **predator.** Everything about me invites you in. My voice, my face, even my smell.

Movie: _____

Scenes: _____

Inane might mean _____

Vile might mean _____

Repulsive might mean _____

Camouflage might mean _____

Predator might mean _____

Hint: "About three things I was **absolutely** positive. First, Edward was a vampire. Second, there was a part of him—and I didn't know how **dominant** that part might be—that thirsted for my blood. And third, I was **unconditionally** and **irrevocably** in love with him."

Solutions

Let's see how you did. Check your answers and write the exact definitions. To help you memorize the vocabulary words, reread the movie excerpts or even act out the scenes with a friend.

Movie: *Twilight,* Summit Entertainment, 2008

Scenes: In the first excerpt, vampires James (Cam Gigandet) and Victoria (Rachelle LeFèvre) are taunting Waylon before he becomes their dinner. In the second excerpt, Edward (Robert Pattinson) has rescued Bella (Kristen Stewart) from thugs in Port Angeles, and in the third excerpt, Edward sparkles in the meadow and shows his true abilities to Bella, who had said that she's not afraid of him.

Inside Scoop: For his role in this film, Robert Pattinson worked out for hours every day and studied how to fight and play baseball. Also, the prom dress that Bella (Kristen Stewart) wore to the prom apparently cost only twenty bucks! See, your mom was right. You don't have to spend a bundle to look great at the prom!

Vocabulary in the Hint: These are the famous lines from the back cover of the first book in the *Twilight* saga. *Absolutely* means *completely*. Synonyms: unconditionally, unmitigatedly, unqualifiedly. *Dominant* means *commanding*. *Unconditionally* means *completely*. *Irrevocably* means *irreversibly*. Synonyms: immutably, peremptorily. Antonym: temporarily.

Inane means *silly* or *foolish*. Synonyms: absurd, asinine, fatuous, puerile, vacuous, vapid.

Vile means *disgusting* or *evil*. Which definition do you think Edward intended? I'd say probably both.

Repulsive means *disgusting*. Synonyms: abhorrent, abominable, execrable, hideous, horrendous, ghastly, grotesque, loathsome, noisome, noxious, repellent, repugnant, revolting, vile.

Camouflage means *disguise*. Synonyms: facade, pretense.

Predator means *hunter*.

Group 64

Here are two excerpts from a movie. See if you can name the movie, describe the scenes, and define the boldface vocabulary words. Check your answers on the following page.

J.: This is not a food baby, all right. I've taken like three pregnancy tests, and I am forshizz up the spout.

LEAH: How did you even generate enough pee for three pregnancy tests? That's amazing.

J.: I don't know. I drank like ten tons of Sunny D. Anyway, dude, I'm telling you I'm pregnant and you're acting shockingly **cavalier.**

Leah: Is this for real? Like for real, for real?

J.: Unfortunately, yes.

_____

LEAH: So, you were bored? That's how this whole blessed miracle came to be?

J.: No, no, no, the act was **premeditated.** I mean the sex, not the whole let's get pregnant thing.

Movie: _____

Scenes: _____

_____

Cavalier might mean _____

_____

Premeditated might mean _____

_____

Hint: "That ain't no Etch A Sketch®. This is one doodle that can't be undid, home skillet."

Solutions

Let's see how you did. Check your answers and write the exact definitions. To help you memorize the vocabulary words, reread the movie excerpts or even act out the scenes with a friend.

Movie: *Juno,* Fox Searchlight Pictures, 2007

Scenes: In the first quote, Juno (Ellen Page) is talking on her novelty hamburger telephone telling Leah (Olivia Thirlby) the news. At first, Leah doesn't believe her and is *cavalier* (overly casual) and responds with the magic question "Honest to blog?" The second quote is from a few minutes later in the movie when they are chatting while moving a living-room set onto Bleeker's (Michael Cera) front lawn. Juno plans to sit in an easy chair in the middle of the tiger rug on Bleeker's lawn when telling him that she's pregnant and that he's the father.

Cavalier means *unconcerned* or *overly casual.* Synonyms: dismissive, flippant, indifferent, insouciant, offhand. *Cavalier* is a pretty high-level word, but if Juno had called Leah *insouciant,* she would have stumped just about everyone watching the movie.

Premeditated means *planned. Pre-* means *before* and *meditate* means *contemplate* or *think,* so *premeditated* means *thought before—planned.* Synonyms: deliberate, intentional.

Group 65

Here's an excerpt from a movie. See if you can name the movie, describe the scene, and define the boldface vocabulary words. Check your answers on the following page.

ELIZABETH: Do you deny it, Mr. Darcy, that you separated a young couple who loved each other, exposing your friend to the **censure** of the world for **caprice** and my sister to its **derision** for disappointed hopes, and involving them both in misery of the **acutest** kind?

MR. DARCY: I do not deny it.

ELIZABETH: How could you do it?

Mr. DARCY: Because I believed you sister **indifferent** to him . . . (*and*) There was, however, I have to admit, the matter of your family . . . It was the lack of **propriety** shown by your mother, your three younger sisters, and even, on occasion, your father.

Movie: _____

Scene: _____

_____

Censure might mean _____

Caprice might mean _____

Derision might mean _____

Acutest might mean _____

Indifferent might mean _____

Propriety might mean _____

Hint: Keira Knightley plays Elizabeth Bennet.

Solutions

Let's see how you did. Check your answers and write the exact definitions. To help you memorize the vocabulary words, reread the movie excerpt or even act out the scene with a friend.

Movie: *Pride & Prejudice,* Focus Features, 2005

Scene: In this scene, Elizabeth Bennett (Keira Knightley) rejects the marriage proposal of Mr. Darcy (Matthew Macfadyen). This movie is absolutely filled with excellent vocabulary; watch it five times and your vocabulary will improve, guaranteed!

Censure means *harsh and official criticism,* like from a judge, society, or the government. Synonyms: admonishment, castigation, condemnation, excoriation, obloquy, opprobrium, rebuke, reprimand, reproach, reproof, vituperation. *Censure* is different than, although related to, *censor,* which means *to edit the content of*—one might **censor** something that is disapproved of or **criticized.**

Caprice means *sudden change of mood or behavior. Capricious* was a synonym for *mercurial* on the *Adventureland* page (Group 34). Synonyms for *capricious:* erratic, fickle, fluctuating, impulsive, inconstant, labile, mercurial, mutable, protean, temperamental, volatile, whimsical. Antonym: stable.

Derision means *insulting ridicule.* Someone who has been **censured** might then be subject to **derision.** Synonyms: contempt, denigration, disdain, disparagement, disrespect, insults, lampooning, satire, scorn.

Acutest means *severest.* Synonyms for *acute:* dire, drastic, dreadful, grave.

Indifferent means *unconcerned* or *uncaring. In-* means *not,* so *indifferent* means *not showing a difference—not caring. Indifferent* was a synonym for *cavalier* on the *Juno* page (Group 64). Synonyms: apathetic, cavalier, dismissive, dispassionate, impassive, insouciant, nonchalant, perfunctory. Standardized tests also use the antonym *solicitous* (concerned), which is the opposite of *indifferent.*

Propriety sounds like *proper* and means *following the **proper** rules of behavior.* Synonyms: decorum, discretion, etiquette, protocol, punctilio, rectitude, refinement. Antonym: indecorum.

Group 66

Here's an excerpt from a movie. See if you can name the movie, describe the scene, and define the boldface vocabulary words. Check your answers on the following page.

> **TAYLOR:** Yes, our culture worshipped the **aggressor** throughout the ages and we end up with spoiled, overpaid, bonehead athletes who contribute little to civilization other than slam dunks and touchdowns. That is the **inevitable** world of . . . But the path of the mind, the path we're on, ours is the path that has brought us these people: Eleanor Roosevelt, Frida Kahlo, Sandra Day O'Connor, Madame Curie, Jane Goodall, Oprah Winfrey and so many others who the world **reveres.**

Movie: _____

Scene: _____

_____

Aggressor might mean _____

_____

Inevitable might mean _____

_____

Reveres might mean _____

_____

Hint: "I will not allow my *Twinkle Town* musicale to be made into **farce.**"

Solutions

Let's see how you did. Check your answers and write the exact definitions. To help you memorize the vocabulary words, reread the movie excerpt or even act out the scene with a friend.

Movie: *High School Musical,* Disney Channel, 2006

Scene: Taylor (Monique Coleman) is trying to convince Gabriella (Vanessa Hudgens) to forget about her feelings for Troy (Zac Efron) and to focus instead on training for the upcoming Scholastic Decathlon competition.

Vocabulary in the Hint: *Farce means mockery, slapstick comedy, or ridiculous situation.*

Aggressor means *the one who attacks first.* Taylor is talking about offensive, rather than defensive, players who **"attack" first.** Synonyms: assailant, instigator.

Inevitable means *unavoidable.* Taylor is pretty well-spoken, but if she were as *articulate* (well-spoken) as Ms. Darbus, she probably would have used the synonym *inexorable* or *ineludible* rather than *inevitable.* Synonyms: fated, ineluctable, ineludible, inexorable, predestined, predetermined.

Reveres means *deeply respects.* Synonyms: esteems, venerates.

Group 67

Here's an excerpt from a movie. See if you can name the movie, describe the scene, and define the boldface vocabulary word. Check your answers on the following page.

WARNER: Elle . . .

ELLE: Yes.

WARNER: One of the reasons I wanted to come here tonight was to discuss our future.

ELLE: And I am fully **amenable** to that discussion . . .

WARNER: Elle, pooh bear, I think we should break up . . .

ELLE: What!?!

WARNER: If I'm going to be a senator, well, I need to marry a Jackie not a Marilyn.

ELLE: So you're breaking up with me because I'm too blonde?!

Movie: _____

Scene: _____

_____

Amenable might mean _____

_____

Hint: One of the taglines for this movie was "Boldly going where no blonde has gone."

Solutions

Let's see how you did. Check your answers and write the exact definition. To help you memorize the vocabulary word, reread the movie excerpt or even act out the scene with a friend.

Movie: *Legally Blonde,* Metro-Goldwyn-Mayer, 2001

Scene: Elle (Reese Witherspoon) and her boyfriend, Warner, are out to dinner. Elle thinks Warner is going to propose, but is shocked when he breaks up with her instead.

Inside Scoop: You might recognize Warner (Matthew Davis) as history teacher Alaric Saltzman on the CW's *Vampire Diaries.*

Amenable means *willing* or *open.* Synonyms: acquiescent, compliant, obliging. I appreciate the clever use of dialogue in this film. The opening scene of Elle and her sorority leads you to imagine her as a fashion-obsessed exercise junky focused only on marrying Warner, but her use of a word like *amenable* hints that she is also *articulate* (well-spoken) and brilliant, as you find out later in the movie. This film is all about believing in yourself. In fact, one of the movie poster taglines for the film was "Believing in yourself NEVER goes out of style!"

Group 68

Here's an excerpt from a movie. See if you can name the movie, describe the scene, and define the boldface vocabulary words. Check your answers on the following page.

ARTHUR: The Lady of the Lake, her arm **clad** in the purest shimmering **samite** held aloft Excalibur from the bosom of the water, signifying by **divine providence** that I, Arthur, was to carry Excalibur. *That* is why I am your king.

DENNIS: Listen, strange women lyin' in ponds distributin' swords is no basis for a system of government. **Supreme executive** power derives from a **mandate** from the masses, not from some **farcical** aquatic ceremony . . . (*Arthur grabs him.*) Come and see the violence **inherent** in the system. Help! Help! I'm being **repressed!**

Movie: _____

Scene: _____

Clad might mean _____

Samite might mean _____

Divine might mean _____

Providence might mean _____

Supreme might mean _____

Executive might mean _____

Mandate might mean _____

Farcical might mean _____

Inherent might mean _____

Repressed might mean _____

Hint: Brave Sir Robin and his minstrels

Solutions

Let's see how you did. Check your answers and write the exact definitions. To help you memorize the vocabulary words, reread the movie excerpt or even act out the scene with a friend.

Movie: *Monty Python and the Holy Grail,* EMI Films, 1975

Scene: At the beginning of this scene, King Arthur (Graham Chapman) is traveling toward a castle and asks Dennis (Michael Palin), a peasant whom he passes, "What knight lives in that castle?" Dennis and his wife were digging filth along the path, but wind up in a heated political argument with Arthur.

Clad means *clothed.*

Samite refers to a *rich silk fabric used in the Middle Ages.*

Divine means *pertaining to God.* It can also mean *noble* or *admirable.*

Providence means *fate* or *the protective care of God.* Synonym: kismet.

Supreme means *highest,* that's why the **Supreme** Court is the highest-ranking court in the United States.

Executive means *lawmaking* or *managerial,* like the **executive** branch of the United States government (which is run by the President) or a corporate **executive.**

Mandate means *formal declaration,* like *mandato* in Spanish, which means *command.* Synonyms: decree, edict, fiat, proclamation.

Farcical means *ridiculous,* and refers to a *farce* (mockery, slapstick comedy, or **ridiculous** situation). Synonyms: absurd, ludicrous, nonsensical, preposterous, risible.

Inherent means *natural* or *inborn.* Synonyms: innate, intrinsic.

Repressed means *put down* or *subdued.* Synonyms: oppressed, subjugated, tyrannized.

Group 69

Here's an excerpt from a movie. See if you can name the movie, describe the scene, and define the boldface vocabulary words. Check your answers on the following page.

JACK: Apparently, there's some sort of high-toned and fancy to-do up at the fort, eh? How could it be that two upstanding gentlemen such as yourselves did not **merit** an invitation?

MURTOGG: Someone has to make sure that this dock stays off-limits to civilians.

JACK: It's a fine goal, to be sure. But it seems to me that a ship like that one makes this one here a bit **superfluous,** really.

MURTOGG: Oh, the *Dauntless* is the power in these waters, true enough. But there's no ship as can match the *Interceptor* for speed.

JACK: I've heard of one, supposed to be very fast, **nigh** uncatchable . . .

Movie: _____

Scene: _____

_____

Merit might mean _____

Superfluous might mean _____

Dauntless might mean _____

Nigh might mean _____

Hint: Johnny Depp created the bizarre way that the main character of this film talks and moves. In fact, he loosely based the character on Rolling Stones guitarist Keith Richards. "Savvy?"

Solutions

Let's see how you did. Check your answers and write the exact definitions. To help you memorize the vocabulary words, reread the movie excerpt or even act out the scene with a friend.

Movie: *Pirates of the Caribbean: The Curse of the Black Pearl,* Walt Disney Pictures, 2003

Scene: Jack Sparrow (Johnny Depp) is at the dock planning to trick the guards who are protecting the *Interceptor* so he can steal the ship.

Inside Scoop: To play this role, Johnny Depp used costumes and smears of charcoal to conceal his many tattoos. Speaking of tats, you can see Orlando Bloom's *Lord of the Rings* tattoo on his right wrist when Will, whom he plays, reaches to touch the medallion on Elizabeth's chest.

Merit means *earn*. *Merit* can also be used as a noun to mean *worthiness of praise*. Synonym: warrant.

Superfluous means *unnecessary* or *more than needed*. In the first *Twilight* book, Alice describes the many vampire weapons and powers—strength, speed, acute senses, attractiveness—to Bella and then states, "We have another fairly superfluous weapon. We're also venomous . . . The venom doesn't kill—it merely incapacitates." The venom is **superfluous** since "if we're that close, the prey doesn't escape." So, the venom is **more than needed** to get the job done. Synonym: redundant.

Dauntless means *fearless*. Synonyms: audacious, doughty, indomitable, intrepid, plucky, resolute, spirited, valiant.

Nigh means *almost* or *near*.

Group  70

Here are three excerpts from a movie. See if you can name the movie, describe the scenes, and define the boldface vocabulary words. Check your answers on the following page.

KATHY: This is not a beauty pageant. This is a scholarship program and it has been ever since my **reign,** and I fully intend on maintaining that **credo.**

VICTOR: In '96 my girl froze like a puddle halfway through her **aria** from *La Bohème*. Afterwards, she told a reporter from *Pageant* magazine that I was a crazed perfectionist who had **harangued** her to within an inch of her sanity. Of course, after that article came out, no one wanted me.

CHERYL: Twirling can be a real art. I saw this girl once, a cheerleader doing it at a football game, and she lit her batons on fire and did this sexy dance. I wish I could do something like that.

GRACIE: Well, why can't you?

CHERYL: Oh, my parents don't like anything **ostentatious,** and they really don't like fire.

Movie: _____

Scenes: _____

Reign might mean _____

Credo might mean _____

Aria might mean _____

Harangued might mean _____

Ostentatious might mean _____

Hint: The title of this movie translates to "Miss Pleasantness."

Solutions

Let's see how you did. Check your answers and write the exact definitions. To help you memorize the vocabulary words, reread the movie excerpts or even act out the scenes with a friend.

Movie: *Miss Congeniality,* Warner Bros., 2000

Scenes: In the first excerpt, Kathy (Candice Bergen), head of the Miss United States contest, corrects Gracie (Sandra Bullock), who incorrectly refers to the contest as a beauty pageant. In the second excerpt, Gracie's pageant mentor, Victor (Michael Caine), explains how he lost his clients. In the third excerpt, Cheryl (Heather Burns), Miss Rhode Island, discusses the talent part of the competition.

Vocabulary in the Hint: *Congeniality* means *friendliness and pleasantness.* The "Miss Congeniality" award is an actual award given at beauty pageants to the participant who is considered "the most congenial, *charismatic* (charming), and inspirational participant." The award is also referred to as "Miss Amity," which gives you your first synonym. The others are *amiability, conviviality, geniality,* and *hospitality.*

Reign means *rule* or *holding of an official title.* Kathy is referring to the year that she won and **held the title** of Miss United States. Synonym: incumbency.

Credo means *declaration of beliefs.* In fact, *cred-* means *believe,* as in *credible* (believable) and *incredulous* (disbelieving). Synonyms: axiom, canon, conviction, creed, doctrine, dogma, ideology, tenet.

Aria means *solo from an opera.*

Harangued means *aggressively pestered or criticized.* Synonym: berated.

Ostentatious refers to *a snobby, showy, or conceited display of wealth, especially in an attempt to impress.* Synonyms: pretentious, showy.

Quiz 7

I. Let's review some of the words that you've seen in Groups 61–70. Match each of the following words to the correct definition or synonym on the right. If you need help, refer back to the movie excerpts and definitions. Then check the solutions on page 238.

1. Septic	A. Immaculate
2. Anarchy	B. Insouciant
3. Pristine	C. Mayhem
4. Inane	D. Putrid
5. Cavalier	E. Sudden change
6. Censure	F. Fatuous
7. Caprice	G. Inexorable
8. Propriety	H. Opprobrium
9. Inevitable	I. Pretentious
10. Revere	J. Rectitude
11. Amenable	K. Indomitable
12. Mandate	L. Venerate
13. Superfluous	M. Acquiescent
14. Dauntless	N. Redundant
15. Ostentatious	O. Fiat

II. Let's review several of the word parts that you've seen in Groups 61–70. Match each of the following word parts to the correct definition or synonym on the right. Then check the solutions on page 238.

16. -Archy (as in *anarchy*)	A. Not
17. Oligo- (as in *oligarchy*)	B. Small number
18. Pre- (as in *premeditated*)	C. Ruler
19. In- (as in *indifferent*)	D. Believe
20. Cred- (as in *credible*)	E. Before

III. Match each group of synonyms to its general meaning. Then check the solutions on page 238.

21. Anarchy   A. Pure
    Bedlam
    Chaos
    Mayhem
    Pandemonium
    Turmoil

22. Immaculate   B. Unconcerned
    Intact
    Pristine

23. Cavalier   C. Willing
    Dismissive
    Flippant
    Indifferent
    Insouciant
    Offhand

24. Admonishment   D. Disorder
    Censure
    Condemnation
    Excoriation
    Opprobrium
    Reproach
    Reproof
    Vituperation

25. Acquiescent   E. Declaration of beliefs
    Amenable
    Compliant
    Obliging

26. Canon   F. Criticism
    Credo
    Doctrine
    Dogma

Here are two excerpts from a movie. See if you can name the movie, describe the scenes, and define the boldface vocabulary words. Check your answers on the following page.

HOPE: You remember in music appreciation we had a class on Mozart? Remember you said he was, like, a musical pod?

REVEREND: **Prodigy.**

HOPE: Exactly. Well, I have one of those, and he's living under my bed!

_____

PROFESSOR: Start with a C-major chord, then a **modulation** to G. Once we get to G, we go back to C, very simple. And we have C, G, C. At the very beginning, C-major chord, . . . we have this **chaotic** evolution into a **remote** G-major.

Movie: _____

Scenes: _____

Prodigy might mean _____

_____

Modulation might mean _____

_____

Chaotic might mean _____

_____

Remote might mean _____

_____

Hint: "Do you know what music is? It's God's little reminder there's something else besides us in this universe: A **harmonic** connection between all living beings, everywhere, even the stars."

Solutions

Let's see how you did. Check your answers and write the exact definitions. To help you memorize the vocabulary words, reread the movie excerpts or even act out the scenes with a friend.

Movie: *August Rush,* Warner Bros., 2007

Scenes: Twelve-year-old August (Freddie Highmore) follows the sounds of music he hears to a church, and then hides and sleeps under a bed in the church. The bed belongs to Hope, a child who lives in the church. In the morning, Hope finds August and introduces him to piano and musical notation. While she goes to school, August plays piano and begins writing down compositions. When Hope gets home from school, she sees what August has done and runs to tell Reverend James. In the second excerpt, August is in class at Juilliard, an elite school for the performing arts.

Inside Scoop: *August Rush* loosely resembles Charles Dickens' *Oliver Twist.*

Vocabulary in the Hint: *Harmonic* means *relating to musical harmony* (notes combined to form a pleasant-sounding whole). Synonyms: dulcet, euphonic, mellifluous, melodious, polyphonic. Antonyms: cacophonous, dissonant.

Prodigy means *genius.* Mozart was a musical prodigy, Galileo was a science prodigy, and Tiger Woods is a golf prodigy. Also, *The Big Bang Theory*'s Sheldon Cooper is a prodigy; with an IQ of 187, he started college when he was 11 years old and finished his PhD at age 15. Synonyms: mastermind, virtuoso, wunderkind.

Modulation means *altering* or *changing, especially in music, from one key to another.*

Chaotic means *disordered.* Synonyms: anarchic, in pandemonium, in turmoil.

Remote means *unlikely* or *far away,* as in your TV **remote** that allows you to change channels from **far away.** So, in music, a **remote** chord is one that is **far away** from another, like C to G. In fact, the opposite of a **remote** modulation between chords is a closely related modulation.

Group 72

Here are two excerpts from a movie. See if you can name the movie, describe the scenes, and define the boldface vocabulary words. Check your answers on the following page.

BROOKS: Son, six wardens have been through here in my **tenure**, and I've learned one **immutable, universal** truth.

_____

ANDY: How can you be so **obtuse?**

WARDEN: What? What did you call me?

ANDY: Obtuse. Is it deliberate?

WARDEN: Son, you are forgetting yourself . . .

ANDY: Sir, if I were to ever get out, I would never mention what goes on here. I'd be just as **indictable** as you for laundering that money.

Movie: _____

Scenes: _____

_____

Tenure might mean _____

Immutable might mean _____

Universal might mean _____

Obtuse might mean _____

Indictable might mean _____

Hint: One of the words in the title of this film can mean *being saved, set free, or forgiven.*

Solutions

Let's see how you did. Check your answers and write the exact definitions. To help you memorize the vocabulary words, reread the movie excerpts or even act out the scenes with a friend.

Movie: *The Shawshank Redemption,* Columbia Pictures, 1994

Scenes: In the first quote, Andy (Tim Robbins), an inmate at Shawshank prison, wants to ask the Warden for funds to buy books for the library, but Brooks' (James Whitmore) "immutable truth" is that the Warden will be too cheap to do it. In the second excerpt, Andy is angry at the Warden for having dismissed new proof of Andy's innocence.

Inside Scoop: *The Shawshank Redemption* was *parodied* (humorously imitated) in the 2009 *Family Guy* episode "Three Kings." Peter plays Andy Dufresne, and Cleveland plays Red (the Morgan Freeman character).

Vocabulary in the Hint: *Redemption* can mean *being saved, set free, or forgiven.* Synonym: absolution.

Tenure means *term of office,* but Brooks is referring to his **term** in prison. Synonym: incumbency. *Tenure* can also mean *assured employment,* such as when a university professor is granted **tenure.**

Immutable means *absolute* or *unchangeable. Im-* means *not,* and *mutable* means *changeable,* so *not changeable.* Synonym: incontrovertible.

Universal means *all-inclusive,* like it applies to every situation in the whole **universe.** Synonyms: omnipresent, ubiquitous. *Omni-* means *all,* and that's why *omnipresent* means *all-present—all-inclusive.*

Obtuse means *slow to comprehend.* Synonyms: dense, thick. Antonym: astute.

Indictable means *able to be charged with a crime.*

Group 73

Here are three excerpts from a movie. See if you can name the movie, describe the scenes, and define the boldface vocabulary words. Check your answers on the following page.

DANIEL: If walking past office was attempt to demonstrate presence of skirt, can only say that it has failed **parlously** . . . **Mortified** to have caused offense. Will avoid all non–PC **overtones** in future.

MARK: I realize that when I met you at the turkey curry buffet that I was unforgivably rude and wearing a reindeer jumper that my mother had given me the day before. But the thing is, what I'm trying to say, very **inarticulately,** is that, um . . . in fact, perhaps, despite appearances, I like you very much . . . just as you are.

MARK: . . . today's verdict has been the result of five years of struggle by this woman, Eleanor Heaney, to save the man she loves from an **extradition** order that would have been **tantamount** to a death sentence.

Movie: _____

Scenes: _____

Parlously might mean _____

Mortified might mean _____

Overtones might mean _____

Inarticulately might mean _____

Extradition might mean _____

Tantamount might mean _____

Hint: "This Year's Resolutions: Stop smoking. Stop drinking. Find inner poise. Go to the gym three times a week. Don't flirt with the boss. Reduce thighs. Learn to love thighs. Forget about thighs."

Solutions

Let's see how you did. Check your answers and write the exact definitions. To help you memorize the vocabulary words, reread the movie excerpts or even act out the scenes with a friend.

Movie: *Bridget Jones's Diary,* Miramax Films, 2001

Scenes: In the first excerpt, Bridget (Renée Zellweger) and Daniel (Hugh Grant) are flirting through email messages. In the second excerpt, Mark (Colin Firth) declares his true feelings for Bridget. And in the third excerpt, Bridget interviews Mark (a lawyer) on her television show.

Inside Scoop: This story is based on Jane Austen's *Pride and Prejudice.* Have you noticed how many modern films are inspired by the works of Jane Austen or William Shakespeare? Here are a few: *Twilight, Clueless, 10 Things I Hate About You, She's The Man, High School Musical, Bridget Jones's Diary,* and *The Hangover.* OK, maybe not *The Hangover,* but the others are indeed modern retellings of classic love stories!

Parlously means *tremendously* or *dangerously* and comes from the word *perilously* (dangerously).

Mortified means *embarrassed.* Have you ever been so embarrassed that you said, "I almost died!" Well, *mort-* means *death,* and that's exactly where the word *mortified* comes from. Synonyms: abashed, chagrined, discomfited.

Overtones means *subtle implications.* Synonyms: connotations, insinuations, intimations, nuances, undertones.

Inarticulately means *unclearly expressed.* Synonyms: incoherently, incomprehensibly, unintelligibly.

Extradition means *moving of a criminal or criminal suspect from one country to another.* Synonyms: deportation, expatriation, repatriation.

Tantamount means *the same as* or *with the same effect as.*

Group 74

Here is an excerpt from a movie. See if you can name the movie, describe the scene, and define the boldface vocabulary words. Check your answers on the following page.

BRIONY TALLIS (AGE 13): Prologue. This is the tale of spontaneous Arabella who ran away with an **extrinsic** fellow. It grieved her parents to see their firstborn **evanesce** from her home to go to Eastbourne.

Movie: _____

Scene: _____

_____

Prologue might mean _____

_____

Extrinsic might mean _____

_____

Evanesce might mean _____

_____

Hint: "Briony found my address somehow and sent a letter. The first surprise was she didn't go up to Cambridge. She's doing nurses' training at my old hospital. I think she may be doing this as some kind of **penance.** She says she's beginning to get the full grasp of what she did and what it meant."

Solutions

Let's see how you did. Check your answers and write the exact definitions. To help you memorize the vocabulary words, reread the movie excerpts or even act out the scenes with a friend.

Movie: *Atonement,* Focus Features, 2007

Scene: Briony (Saoirse Ronan), at age thirteen, writes *fanciful* (imaginative) stories and plays. In the excerpt, Briony is narrating the *prologue* (introduction) for a play that she and her cousins are rehearsing.

Inside Scoop: *InStyle* magazine calls the green silk dress that Keira Knightley (playing Cecilia) wears in the film, "the best film costume of all time." The now-famous dress is bias cut with twisted shoulder straps and no back. Knightley wore several copies during filming, one of which later garnered $46,000 at a charity auction.

Vocabulary in the Hint: *Penance* means *self-punishment for having committed a wrong or sin* and is a synonym for ***atonement,*** the film's title. Other synonyms are *amends, contrition,* and *expiation.* Briony is **atoning** for having wrongly accused Robbie, the housekeeper's son, of a crime.

Prologue means *introduction.* Synonyms: exordium, foreword, preamble, preface, prelude, proem. Antonym: epilogue.

Extrinsic means *from outside,* and *ex-* means *out,* as in *exit, excursion,* and *ex-boyfriend.* Briony means that the fellow was an **outsider** (from somewhere else) and Arabella **evanesced** (disappeared) from her home to go live with him.

Evanesce means *disappear.* The related word and standardized test favorite, *evanescent,* means *about to disappear.* Synonyms for *evanescent*: ephemeral, fleeting, fugitive, transient, transitory. Antonyms: eternal, permanent.

Here are two excerpts from a movie. See if you can name the movie, describe the scenes, and define the boldface vocabulary words. Check your answers on the following page.

Ms. Kornblut (Dog Trainer): "**Incorrigible.**" I don't believe in that word. Every dog wants to learn . . . Even an **unruly** dog likes to obey his leader . . . *(She takes the dog for a walk, but he runs away. So she blows her whistle. The dog charges back, tackles her, and vehemently humps her leg.)* That's it! He is out!

John: I'm sorry, he usually only does this with poodles.

Ms. Kornblut: That dog is a bad influence on the others. Now, leg humping is like a virus once it takes hold of the group. No, he has got to go.

John: I thought it was maybe your hair. It reminded him of a poodle.

Ms. Kornblut: Never bring him back.

_____

John: I want a moment of silence just to take this in, OK, before the **pandemonium.**

Movie: _____

Scenes: _____

_____

Incorrigible might mean _____

Unruly might mean _____

Pandemonium might mean _____

Hint: "Give her a Labrador. It's supposed to be just like kids, only easier to train."

Solutions

Let's see how you did. Check your answers and write the exact definitions. To help you memorize the vocabulary words, reread the movie excerpts or even act out the scenes with a friend.

Movie: *Marley & Me,* 20th Century Fox, 2008

Scenes: In the first excerpt, John (Owen Wilson) and Jenny (Jennifer Aniston) take their dog, Marley, to obedience school. As the excerpt shows, they get kicked out and permanently banned. In the second excerpt, John, Jenny, their three kids, and Marley pull into their new home in peaceful, residential Pennsylvania. Marley creates his characteristic *pandemonium* (noisy disorder) by immediately breaking the concrete birdbath on the front porch.

Inside Scoop: Twenty-two different dogs, all yellow Labrador Retrievers, play the part of Marley.

Incorrigible means *not able to be corrected or reformed,* and, in fact, *in-* means *not* and *corrigible* means *correctable,* like *corregible* in Spanish. Marley is indeed pretty **incorrigible,** chewing everything from the floor tiles to the ear on Colleen's stuffed lamb toy. Synonyms: inveterate, irredeemable.

Unruly means *undisciplined* or *disorderly*—without **rul**es. Marley showed Ms. Kornblut who's boss! Synonyms: boisterous, contumacious, disobedient, intractable, irrepressible, obstreperous, rambunctious, recalcitrant, refractory, restive, willful.

Pandemonium means *noisy disorder.* Synonyms: anarchy, bedlam, chaos, commotion, furor, hubbub, hullabaloo, mayhem, rumpus, tumult, turmoil, uproar.

Group 76

Here's an excerpt from a movie. See if you can name the movie, describe the scene, and define the boldface vocabulary word. Check your answers on the following page.

TYLER: (reporting to the Maryland School of Arts for his community service hours) I'm Tyler Gage. I'm here . . .

SCHOOL DIRECTOR: Come in, Mr. Gage. Take a seat . . . Well, I see that you're overwhelmed with **remorse.** You have no idea of the consequences of your actions, do you?

TYLER: Yeah, two hundred hours.

SCHOOL DIRECTOR: Actually, there's a little more to it. Most of our students are here on scholarship. The cost of repairing the damage that you did is roughly the equivalent of one student's tuition.

Movie: _____

Scene: _____

_____

Remorse might mean _____

_____

Hint: Channing Tatum

Solutions

Let's see how you did. Check your answers and write the exact definition. To help you memorize the vocabulary word, reread the movie excerpt or even act out the scene with a friend.

Movie: *Step Up,* Touchstone Pictures, 2006

Scene: Tyler (Channing Tatum) has been sentenced to serve 200 hours of community service for breaking into the Maryland School of Arts and destroying the set of a play. In the excerpt, Tyler reports to the school to serve the hours and meets the school's director.

Inside Scoop: The impressive chemistry between Channing Tatum and his costar, Jenna Dewan, is the real deal. They met while making *Step Up* and were married in 2009.

Remorse means *regret for wrongdoing.* Synonyms: compunction, contrition, penitence, repentance, ruefulness. Later in the excerpt, the school director says that Tyler does not realize the consequences of the damage that he did to the school. A terrific high-level synonym for *consequences* that I've seen quite often on standardized tests is *ramifications.*

Here are three excerpts from a movie. See if you can name the movie, describe the scenes, and define the boldface vocabulary words. Check your answers on the following page.

CHER: Yuk! Uh, the **maudlin** music of the University station? Waa, waa, waa! What is it about college and cry-baby music?

———————————

HEATHER: Oh Josh, please. He's taken our minds at the most **fecund** point and restrained them before they've wandered through the garden of ideas. It's just like Hamlet said, "To thine own self be true."

CHER: No, ah, Hamlet didn't say that.

HEATHER: I think that I remember Hamlet accurately.

CHER: Well, I remember Mel Gibson accurately, and he didn't say that. That Polonius guy did.

———————————

CHER: Going all the way is like a really big decision. I can't believe I was so **capricious** about it. Dee, I almost had sex with him.

Movie: _____

Scenes: _____

_____

Maudlin might mean _____

Fecund might mean _____

Capricious might mean _____

Hint: This movie features a young Paul Rudd in his first year of making movies, which was almost a decade before his hilarious roles in *Anchorman, Forgetting Sarah Marshall, Role Models, Knocked Up,* and *I Love You, Man.*

Solutions

Let's see how you did. Check your answers and write the exact definitions. To help you memorize the vocabulary words, reread the movie excerpts or even act out the scenes with a friend.

Movie: *Clueless,* Paramount Pictures, 1995

Scenes: Cher (Alicia Silverstone) is **clueless** to her true feelings for Josh (Paul Rudd) and often spars with him, such as complaining about his music in the first excerpt. In the second excerpt, she corrects Josh's girlfriend, who misquotes Hamlet. And in the third excerpt, still oblivious to her feelings for Josh, she complains to Dionne and Murray that she almost had sex with Christian.

Inside Scoop: If you re-watch this movie, you'll recognize Dionne's boyfriend, Murray, played by Donald Faison, who is now famous as Dr. Turk on *Scrubs!*

Maudlin means *overly sentimental* or even *self-pitying.* Synonyms: cloying, hokey, lachrymose, mawkish, mushy, saccharine, treacly.

Fecund means *fertile.* Heather means that their minds are **fertile** in the sense that they are imaginative and ready for and open to the **growth** of new ideas.

Capricious means *changing too quickly or easily.* Synonyms: erratic, fickle, fluctuating, impulsive, inconstant, labile, mercurial, mutable, protean, temperamental, volatile, whimsical. Antonym: stable. You can remember the synonym *mercurial* by thinking of the planet Mercury, the fastest-moving planet, which is named for the Roman god of messengers. You can see the connection between **moving fast** and **changing too quickly.**

Here's an excerpt from a movie. See if you can name the movie, describe the scene, and define the boldface vocabulary word. Check your answers on the following page.

LEIGH ANNE: Look, here's the deal. I don't need y'all to approve my choices, all right? But I do ask that you respect them. You've *no* idea what this boy's been through, and if this is going to become some running **diatribe,** I can find an overpriced salad a lot closer to home.

Movie: _____

Scene: _____

_____

Diatribe might mean _____

_____

Hint: Actual college football coaches Phillip Fulmer, Lou Holtz, Houston Nutt, Ed Orgeron, Nick Saban, and Tommy Tuberville appear in this movie.

Solutions

Let's see how you did. Check your answers and write the exact definition. To help you memorize the vocabulary word, reread the movie excerpt or even act out the scene with a friend.

Movie: *The Blind Side,* Warner Bros., 2009

Scene: Leigh Anne (Sandra Bullock) has taken in a homeless teenager, Michael Oher (Quinton Aaron). In this scene, Leigh Anne is having lunch with friends who make jokes about Michael. The jokes become harsh and even racist, and Leigh Anne gets offended and delivers this scathing *retort* (sharp answer).

Inside Scoop: Did you notice Robert Pattinson of *Twilight* in this film? When Leigh Anne comes home for the first time with Michael Oher, her daughter Collins is on the couch wearing a green mud mask, watching a movie, and talking on her pink cell phone saying "I know, it's my favorite part. *So* cute." In the background, on Collins' television set, you can catch a quick glimpse of Robert Pattinson in his role as Edward in *Twilight!*

Diatribe means *angry, attacking speech.* Synonyms: broadside, fulmination, harangue, invective, onslaught, philippic, polemic, rant, tirade.

Group 79

Here are two excerpts from a movie. See if you can name the movie, describe the scenes, and define the boldface vocabulary words. Check your answers on the following page.

ED HARKEN: A lot of you have been hearing the **affiliates** complaining about a lack of **diversity** on the news team.

CHAMP KIND: What in the hell's "diversity"?

RON: Well, I could be wrong, but I believe, ahh, *Diversity* is an old, old wooden ship that was used during the Civil War era.

RON: (*singing terribly*) Skyrockets in flight . . . Afternoon delight . . . and . . . I make fart noises with my mouth. And I like to cook . . .

BARTENDER: Hey, nut job, quit the singing! You're creeping out all the regulars . . .

RON: I'm expressing my inner **anguish** through the **majesty** of song.

Movie: _____

Scenes: _____

_____

Affiliates might mean _____

Diversity might mean _____

Anguish might mean _____

Majesty might mean _____

Hint: "Everyone just relax, all right? Believe me, if there's one thing Ron Burgundy knows, it's women."

Solutions

Let's see how you did. Check your answers and write the exact definitions. To help you memorize the vocabulary words, reread the movie excerpts or even act out the scenes with a friend.

Movie: *Anchorman: The Legend of Ron Burgundy,* DreamWorks, 2004

Scenes: In the first excerpt, Ron's boss, Ed Harken (Fred Willard), is preparing the news team for the announcement that a woman (Christina Applegate) is being added to the team. Ron Burgundy (Will Ferrell) responds with his classic buffoonery. In the second excerpt, Ron is down and out in a bar three months after he's been fired and just before Ed calls him back in to anchor at a live panda birth.

Affiliates means *individuals joined as a group.* TV affiliates are independent stations that are part of a network. The word *affiliate* comes from *filius* meaning *son*. This definition sounds just like something Ron Burgundy would make up, but the meaning is actually true. *Filius* can help you remember the high-level SAT word *filial* (of a **son** or daughter).

Diversity means *variety.* Synonyms: array, heterogeneity, mélange, multifariousness, multiplicity, variegation. That is a terrific list of synonyms; I have seen almost every one of these words on tests. Memorize them and your standardized test scores will go up!

Anguish means *extreme pain.* Synonyms: agony, desolation, despair, despondency, wretchedness. Ron is in anguish because he was fired from the news team, dumped by his girlfriend, and abandoned by his friends.

Majesty means *dignity, power,* or *beauty.*

Here are three excerpts from a movie. See if you can name the movie, describe the scenes, and define the boldface vocabulary words. Check your answers on the following page.

MINISTER: Let us be thankful today that a young life was saved by our Lord. And let us pray for the lives of the others involved who are clearly not on the path of **righteousness.**

LANDON: You sit at lunch table 7, which isn't exactly the reject table, but is definitely in self-**exile** territory. You have exactly one sweater. You like to look at your feet when you walk. Oh, oh, and yeah, for fun, you like to tutor on weekends and hang out with the cool kids from "Stars and Planets." Now, how does that sound?

JAMIE: Thoroughly predictable, nothing I haven't heard before.

LANDON: You don't care what people think about you?

JAMIE: No.

LANDON: I brought a thermos of hot coffee and a blanket . . .

JAMIE: Are you trying to seduce me?

LANDON: Why, are you seducible? *(Jamie shakes her head "no.")* That's what I thought. **Ergo,** a second blanket. One for me, one for you.

Movie: _____

Scenes: _____

Righteousness might mean _____

Exile might mean _____

Ergo might mean _____

Hint: "Jamie saved my life. She taught me everything . . . about life, hope, and the long journey ahead. I'll always miss her."

Solutions

Let's see how you did. Check your answers and write the exact definitions. To help you memorize the vocabulary words, reread the movie excerpts or even act out the scenes with a friend.

Movie: *A Walk to Remember,* Warner Bros., 2002

Scenes: In the first excerpt, during a sermon, Reverend Sullivan (Peter Coyote) chides Landon (Shane West) for his involvement in a prank that left a classmate hurt. In the second excerpt, Landon and Jamie (Mandy Moore) flirt on the school bus, and in the third excerpt, Landon and Jamie are out late at night waiting to see Pluto through Jamie's telescope.

Righteousness means *morality*. You heard the word *righteous* from Edward Cullen in *New Moon* (Group 1). You also learned it as a synonym for *virtue* from the *Pride & Prejudice* excerpt (Group 11) and from the word *self-righteous* (with a superior attitude) in the *10 Things I Hate About You* excerpt (Group 33). Someone who is self-righteous thinks that they are always **morally** correct and superior to others. Synonyms for *righteousness*: rectitude, virtue. The opposite of *righteousness* is *vicefulness* (immorality).

Exile means *banishment*. Synonym: expatriation.

Ergo means *therefore*. Synonyms: consequently, hence, whence.

Quiz 8

I. Let's review some of the words that you've seen in Groups 71–80. Match each of the following words to the correct definition or synonym on the right. If you need help, refer back to the movie excerpts and definitions. Then check the solutions on page 238.

1. Prodigy	A. Incontrovertible
2. Tenure	B. Thick
3. Immutable	C. Virtuoso
4. Universal	D. Term
5. Obtuse	E. Atonement
6. Penance	F. Ubiquitous
7. Extrinsic	G. Inveterate
8. Evanesce	H. Mawkish
9. Incorrigible	I. Mercurial
10. Unruly	J. From outside
11. Maudlin	K. Disappear
12. Fecund	L. Obstreperous
13. Capricious	M. Rectitude
14. Righteousness	N. Banishment
15. Exile	O. Fertile

II. Let's review several of the word parts that you've seen in Groups 71–80. Match each of the following word parts to the correct definition or synonym on the right. Then check the solutions on page 238.

16. Omni- (as in *omnipresent*)	A. Death
17. Mort- (as in *mortified*)	B. Out
18. Ex- (as in *extrinsic*)	C. Not
19. In- (as in *incorrigible*)	D. Son
20. Filius (as in *filial*)	E. All

III. Match each group of synonyms to its general meaning. Then check the solutions on page 238.

21. Ephemeral
    Evanescent
    Fleeting
    Fugitive
    Transitory

    A. Undisciplined and disorderly

22. Boisterous
    Contumacious
    Intractable
    Irrepressible
    Obstreperous
    Recalcitrant
    Refractory
    Restive
    Unruly

    B. Disrespect

23. Audacity
    Cheek
    Effrontery
    Impertinence
    Impudence
    Insolence
    Temerity

    C. Disappearing

24. Acute
    Astute
    Canny
    Incisive
    Judicious
    Keen
    Perspicacious
    Sagacious
    Savvy
    Shrewd

    D. Sharp, smart

Group 81

Here are two excerpts from a movie. See if you can name the movie, describe the scenes, and define the boldface vocabulary words. Check your answers on the following page.

MR. BINGLEY: I know this is all very **untoward**, but I would like to request the privilege of speaking to Miss Bennet, alone . . . (*now alone with Jane Bennet*) First, I must tell you I've been the most **unmitigated**, incomprehensive ass.

JANE: He thought me **indifferent.**

ELIZABETH: Unfathomable.

JANE: No doubt poisoned by his **pernicious** sister.

Movie: _____

Scenes: _____

_____

Untoward might mean _____

Unmitigated might mean _____

Indifferent might mean _____

Unfathomable might mean _____

Pernicious might mean _____

Hint: A *Bollywood* (Hindi cinema) adaptation of this classic love story is called *Bride and Prejudice*.

Solutions

Let's see how you did. Check your answers and write the exact definitions. To help you memorize the vocabulary words, reread the movie excerpts or even act out the scenes with a friend.

Movie: *Pride & Prejudice,* Focus Features, 2005

Scenes: In the first excerpt, Mr. Bingley (Simon Woods) returns to the Bennet house to apologize to Jane for having earlier ended their relationship and to ask her to marry him. She replies tearfully, "A thousand times, yes!" In the second excerpt, Jane and her sister, Elizabeth (Keira Knightley), are discussing Mr. Bingley and why he had previously left.

Inside Scoop: Rosamund Pike, the actress who plays Jane Bennet, does a terrific job portraying Jane as sweet, beautiful, and simple-minded. In real life, actress Rosamund Pike may be sweet and beautiful, but she's definitely not simple-minded—she graduated with honors from Oxford University; speaks English, German, and French; and plays the piano and cello!

Untoward means *inconvenient* or *inappropriate*. Synonyms: improper, infelicitous, malapropos.

Unmitigated means *complete*. Synonyms: absolute, categorical, consummate, unconditional, unequivocal, unqualified, untempered.

Indifferent means *unconcerned* or *uncaring*. *In-* means *not,* so *indifferent* means *not showing a difference—not caring*. Synonyms: apathetic, cavalier, dismissive, dispassionate, impassive, insouciant, nonchalant, perfunctory. The SAT also loves testing the antonym *solicitous* (concerned), which is the opposite of *indifferent*.

Unfathomable means *impossible to understand*. *Un-* means *not,* and *fathomable* means *understandable,* so *unfathomable* means *not understandable*. Synonyms: enigmatic, impenetrable, inscrutable.

Pernicious means *destructive* or *wicked*. Synonyms: baleful, deleterious, detrimental, inimical, insidious, maleficent, malevolent, malignant, nefarious, noxious. The synonym *maleficent* makes me think of the **wicked** fairy godmother, named Maleficent, in Disney's *Sleeping Beauty*. Antonym: benevolent.

Group 82

Here are three excerpts from a movie. See if you can name the movie, describe the scenes, and define the boldface vocabulary words. Check your answers on the following page.

RON: Really? Strapping guy like you? You've got more of a Beater's build, don't you think? Keeper needs to be quick, **agile.**

CORMAC: (*catches a fly with his fingers*) I like my chances.

———————

SLUGHORN: Farewell, Aragog, king of the **arachnids.** Your body will decay . . . but your spirit lingers on and your human friends find **solace** . . .

———————

LAVENDER: Don't worry, Won-Won! I'm here. I'm here . . .

ALBUS: Oh, to be young and to feel love's **keen** sting.

Movie: _____

Scenes: _____

_____

Agile might mean _____

Arachnids might mean _____

Solace might mean _____

Keen might mean _____

Hint: The name of one of the villains in this film resembles the *draconic,* meaning *excessively severe.* And the name of his boss, the main villain, translates from French as *flight of death.*

Solutions

Let's see how you did. Check your answers and write the exact definitions. To help you memorize the vocabulary words, reread the movie excerpts or even act out the scenes with a friend.

Movie: *Harry Potter and the Half-Blood Prince,* Warner Bros. Pictures, 2009

Scenes: In the first excerpt, Cormac McLaggen (Freddie Stroma) tells Ron (Rupert Grint) that he's going out for Ron's position on the Gryffindor Quidditch (a sport played by wizards and witches) team. In the second excerpt, Professor Slughorn (Jim Broadbent) speaks at Aragog's funeral, and in the third excerpt, Lavender Brown (Jessie Cave) is visiting Ron and doting on him in the infirmary when Ron, mostly unconscious, croaks "Her . . . my . . . nee. Hermione . . . " Hermione (Emma Watson) is thrilled and lovingly takes his hand, but Lavender runs out of the room sobbing.

Vocabulary in the Hint: *Draco Malfoy's* name might come from *draconian* (excessively harsh and severe, especially regarding enforcing laws). *Voldemort,* the main villain, breaks down to *Vol* (flight), *de* (of), *mort* (death).

Agile means *able to move quickly.* Synonyms: fleet-footed, limber, lithe, nimble, supple.

Arachnids refers to *spiders, scorpions, mites, and ticks*, though people usually mean just spiders. Aragog was, of course, Hagrid's (Robbie Coltrane) pet Acromantula (giant, talking spider) who lived in the Forbidden Forest.

Solace means *comfort.* Synonym: consolation, succor.

Keen means *sharp* or *penetrating. Keen* can also mean *eager* or *intelligent.*

Group 83

Here are three excerpts from a movie. See if you can name the movie, describe the scenes, and define the boldface vocabulary words. Check your answers on the following page.

MIRANDA: But, what you don't know is that that sweater is not just blue. It's not **turquoise**. It's not **lapis**. It's actually **cerulean**. And you're also **blithely** unaware of the fact that in 2002 Oscar de la Renta did a collection of cerulean gowns . . .

_____

DOUG: Fashion is not about **utility**. An **accessory** is merely a piece of **iconography** used to express individual identity.

_____

CHRISTIAN: Come on, you hate her, just admit it to me. She's a **notorious** sadist, and not in a good way.

Movie: _____

Scenes: _____

Turquoise might mean _____

Lapis might mean _____

Cerulean might mean _____

Blithely might mean _____

Utility might mean _____

Accessory might mean _____

Iconography might mean _____

Notorious might mean _____

Hint: Meryl Streep enters her first scene of this film carrying a Prada handbag.

Solutions

Let's see how you did. Check your answers and write the exact definitions. To help you memorize the vocabulary words, reread the movie excerpts or even act out the scenes with a friend.

Movie: *The Devil Wears Prada,* 20th Century Fox, 2006

Scenes: In the first excerpt, Miranda (Meryl Streep) reams out her new assistant, Andy (Anne Hathaway). In the second excerpt, Andy has given Lily (Tracie Thoms) a new Marc Jacobs handbag, which Lily and Doug (Rich Sommer) are discussing. In the third excerpt, Andy and Christian (Simon Baker) discuss Miranda.

Turquoise means *greenish-blue,* like the color of the semiprecious gemstone of the same name. Synonym: aquamarine.

Lapis means *deep blue.* Synonym: ultramarine.

Cerulean means *sky blue.* Synonym: azure. Now you know *turquoise, aquamarine, lapis, ultramarine, cerulean,* and *azure.* Use these to spice up your creative or descriptive essays in school—they're more interesting and more specific than just saying "blue." Plus, now you'll know exactly what to expect when you order clothes from a catalog!

Blithely means *with insensitive cheerfulness and lack of concern.*

Utility means *usefulness.* Synonyms: efficacy, productiveness.

Accessory means *add-on,* like a belt or scarf **adds on** to an outfit. Synonyms: adjunct, adornment, appendage, appurtenance, embellishment, frill, trimming. *Accessory* can also mean *someone who assists a criminal in committing a crime.*

Iconography in this case means *images associated with a style*, for example, as Doug says, "to express individual identity." *Iconography* can also mean *the study of images and symbols,* which is why Robert Langdon, the main character in *The Da Vinci Code,* is an *iconographer* (one who studies cultural and religious images and symbols).

Notorious looks like *notable* and means *well known for bad things*. Synonym: infamous.

Group 84

Here are two excerpts from a movie. See if you can name the movie, describe the scenes, and define the boldface vocabulary words. Check your answers on the following page.

> **STAINER:** OK, anyway, I love Kirky, but let's face it, the guy's a five.
>
> **DEVON:** Stainer, that's just dirty pool. He's at least a six.
>
> **STAINER:** Six!? All right, you go ahead and pump rainbows into his . . . but I'm just being honest.
>
> **JACK:** Come on, cut him some slack. Look, half a point 'cause he's a nice guy, right, and he's funny, so that's half a point each. That brings him to six. Devon's right . . .
>
> **STAINER:** Meanwhile this Molly is a hard ten, and that five-point **disparity,** that is a **chasm** . . . You can't jump more than two points . . .

> **STAINER:** I'm a six . . . But I get a one-point bump 'cause I'm in a band.
>
> **KIRK:** Stainer, you're in a Hall and Oats cover band. I'm pretty sure that's a deduction.
>
> **STAINER:** Adult Education is a **tribute** band.

Movie: _____

Scenes: _____

_____

Disparity might mean _____

Chasm might mean _____

Tribute might mean _____

Hint: "Fare thee well, dear princess, until our magic carpets **alight** from Agribah to the Cave of Wonders for a night of romance and hockey."

Solutions

Let's see how you did. Check your answers and write the exact definitions. To help you memorize the vocabulary words, reread the movie excerpts or even act out the scenes with a friend.

Movie: *She's Out of My League,* Paramount Pictures, 2010

Scenes: In these two scenes, Kirk (Jay Baruchel) and the guys are bowling and analyzing whether Molly (Alice Eve) could possibly be into Kirk. I like the ultimate message of this movie—as Devon (Nate Torrence) says, " . . . this system is ridiculous. If someone really loves you, then you *are* a ten."

Inside Scoop: You might recognize Alice Eve as jiggling Irish nanny, Erin, from *Sex and the City 2.* And did you recognize Jack (Mike Vogel) as Eric, the soccer coach that Bridget seduces in *Sisterhood of the Traveling Pants?*

Vocabulary in the Hint: *Alight* means *land,* as in "the plane will alight on the runway."

Disparity means *large difference. Dis-* means *not,* and *parity* means *equality,* so *not equal—different.* Synonyms: discrepancy, divergence, gap, variance.

Chasm means *deep crack* or *gap.* Synonyms: abyss, breach, cleft, crevasse, crevice, fault, fissure, fracture, rift, rupture, schism.

Tribute means *something that honors.* The movie *Across the Universe* is a tribute to The Beatles. Synonyms: homage, paean.

Group 85

Here are two excerpts from a movie. See if you can name the movie, describe the scenes, and define the boldface vocabulary words. Check your answers on the following page.

ALEX: Cora is back in town tomorrow and wants to meet us at her studio to work on the song. And, um, she wants to know if we like wheatgrass.

SOPHIE: Sounds **ominous**.

_____

SOPHIE: I appreciate that you bring your own special thought to the music, but I really and honestly feel that we're **pandering**.

ALEX: Which means _trying to make others like you,_ which I personally think is a really nice thing. I do a lot of it myself . . .

SOPHIE: The song is about the struggle, you know, to show your true feelings. And your very confident sexual display is, you know, a total contradiction to the fear and insecurity.

Movie: _____

Scenes: _____

_____

Ominous might mean _____

_____

Pandering might mean _____

_____

Hint: "PoP was one of the biggest bands of the '80s . . . But here's a question: Can you remember the name of the other guy in PoP? What ever happened to Alex Fletcher? Tonight we find out on _Battle of the '80s Has-Beens._"

Solutions

Let's see how you did. Check your answers and write the exact definitions. To help you memorize the vocabulary words, reread the movie excerpts or even act out the scenes with a friend.

Movie: *Music and Lyrics,* Warner Bros. Pictures, 2007

Scenes: Alex Fletcher (Hugh Grant), a professional songwriter, is collaborating with his new writing partner, Sophie (Drew Barrymore), to write a song for Cora, reigning rock superstar. In the first excerpt, Alex relays news to Sophie that Cora is in town, and in the second excerpt, Sophie tries to criticize Cora's changes to their song.

Inside Scoop: Hugh Grant and Drew Barrymore did all of their own singing in the film.

Ominous means *threatening.* Synonyms: foreboding, inauspicious, menacing.

Pandering means *giving in to the immoral desires of others.* Sophie is upset because she wrote a heartfelt love song that Cora is performing while wearing a thong. As Alex says in the excerpt, people pander to make others like them, and in fact, *pandering* makes me think of the word *obsequious,* which you learned from the *Miss Congeniality* scene in Group 30. *Obsequious* and its synonyms *fawning, ingratiating, oleaginous, servile, sycophantic,* and *toady* mean *excessively flattering or obedient,* like a "brownnoser" or "suck-up."

Group 86

Here are three excerpts from a movie. See if you can name the movie, describe the scenes, and define the boldface vocabulary words. Check your answers on the following page.

HAMPTON ROTH: Listen to the **truncated** bastard language of today. The average vocabulary is a third of what it was a hundred years ago.

———————

HAMPTON ROTH: I am about the love, as you know. That's why you keep me around, to keep that **rampant, rapacious** ambition of yours in check. (*to Will*) I have a thought! Why don't you use that newly acquired **scintilla** of power and influence to get Summer here to write an article about your man Robredo? That way Summer gets a break, and you get the word out.

———————

MAYA: I really like Summer. I can't believe she turned out to be such a . . .

WILL: Heartbreaker?

MAYA: No.

WILL: Opportunist?

Movie: _____

Scenes: _____

Truncated might mean _____

Rampant might mean _____

Rapacious might mean _____

Scintilla might mean _____

Opportunist might mean _____

Hint: Isla Fisher, Rachel Weisz, Elizabeth Banks, and Ryan Reynolds

Solutions

Let's see how you did. Check your answers and write the exact definitions. To help you memorize the vocabulary words, reread the movie excerpts or even act out the scenes with a friend.

Movie: *Definitely, Maybe,* Universal Pictures, 2008

Scenes: Will's (Ryan Reynolds) daughter, Maya (Abigail Breslin), asks him to tell her the story of how he met her mother. He makes the story a game by changing the names of the women to let Maya figure out which one is her mother. In the first excerpt, Professor Hampton Roth (Kevin Kline) is giving a lecture about the *degradation* (deterioration) of vocabulary. In the second excerpt, Hampton sets up Summer (Rachel Weisz) with Will, and in the third excerpt, Maya, comments on Will's story.

Inside Scoop: This movie was named after the Oasis album *Definitely Maybe*.

Truncated means *shortened.* Synonyms: abbreviated, curtailed.

Rampant means *uncontrolled.* Synonym: unchecked.

Rapacious means *aggressively greedy.* Synonyms: acquisitive, avaricious, covetous, insatiable, mercenary, predatory. Antonyms: generous, munificent.

Scintilla means *a tiny bit.* Synonyms: iota, modicum, particle.

Opportunist means *a person who uses **opportunities** to his or her selfish advantage.*

Group 87

Here are two excerpts from a movie. See if you can name the movie, describe the scenes, and define the boldface vocabulary words. Check your answers on the following page.

RICHARD: Dwayne has a goal. He has a dream. It may not be my dream. It may not be yours. But he's pursuing it with great **conviction** and focus. In fact, I was thinking about the nine steps . . .

_____

FRANK: (*helping push a VW bus to get it into gear*) I just want everyone here to know that I am the **preeminent** Proust scholar in the United States.

Movie: _____

Scenes: _____

_____

Conviction might mean _____

_____

Preeminent might mean _____

_____

Hint: Steve Carell plays Frank.

Solutions

Let's see how you did. Check your answers and write the exact definitions. To help you memorize the vocabulary words, reread the movie excerpts or even act out the scenes with a friend.

Movie: *Little Miss Sunshine,* Fox Searchlight Pictures, 2006

Scenes: In the first excerpt, Richard (Greg Kinnear) says he's proud of Dwayne's (Paul Dano) vow of silence. In the second excerpt, Frank (Steve Carell) thinks it's funny that he, the foremost Proust scholar in the United States, is pushing a beat-up VW bus.

Inside Scoop: Olive (Abigail Breslin) performs in the beauty pageant to Rick James' song "Super Freak."

Conviction means *firm belief* and comes from the word *convince;* when you have *conviction,* you are totally *convinced—you're sure.* Of course, it can also refer to *a jury's pronouncement of guilt.* Synonym: certitude.

Preeminent means *greatest* or *most important.* Synonyms: foremost, illustrious, marquee, supreme.

Group 88

Here is an excerpt from a movie. See if you can name the movie, describe the scene, and define the boldface vocabulary word. Check your answers on the following page.

IRIS: (*narrating the opening scene*) For some, quite inexplicably, love fades; for others, love is simply lost. But then, of course, love can also be found, even if just for the night. And then there's another kind of love, the cruelest kind. The one that almost kills its victims. It's called **unrequited** love. Of that I am an expert. Most love stories are about people who fall in love with each other. But what about . . . those of us who fall in love alone? We are the victims of the one-sided affair. We are the cursed of the loved ones. We are the unloved ones, the walking wounded . . . These years that I have been in love have been the darkest days of my life. All because I've been cursed by being in love with a man who does not and will not love me back.

Movie: _____   _____

Scene: _____

_____

Unrequited might mean _____

_____

Hint: A house swap between Los Angeles and Surrey, England.

Solutions

Let's see how you did. Check your answers and write the exact definition. To help you memorize the vocabulary word, reread the movie excerpt or even act out the scene with a friend.

Movie: *The Holiday*, Columbia Pictures, 2006

Scene: Iris (Kate Winslet) narrates the opening of the film. She has been in love with Jasper (not Cullen) for three years and is miserable. A short holiday to Los Angeles changes everything.

Inside Scoop: If you're looking for a great book to read, check out the stack that Amanda (Cameron Diaz) brought on her plane ride to England. Her pile includes *The Kite Runner* by Khaled Hosseini, *The Power of Now* by Eckhart Tolle, *Atonement* by Ian McEwan, *Harry Potter and the Sorcerer's Stone* by J. K. Rowling, and *The Wisdom of Forgiveness* by the Dalai Lama.

Unrequited means *not returned*. Synonym: unreciprocated. Notice that *unrequited* is described in the paragraph: " . . . those of us who fall in love alone? We are the victims of the one-sided affair . . . All because I've been cursed by being in love with a man who does not and will not love me back." Figuring out the meaning of a word in context is a great skill to use on SAT, ACT, GED, and GRE reading comprehension questions; they always define difficult words in context. So, when you're unsure of the meaning of a word, read the words and sentences around it.

Group 89

Here are two excerpts from a movie. See if you can name the movie, describe the scenes, and define the boldface vocabulary words. Check your answers on the following page.

HARVARD ADMISSIONS CHAIRMAN: (*reviewing Elle Woods' application to Harvard Law School*) She also designed a line of **faux**-fur panties for her sorority's charity project.

HARVARD ADMISSIONS OFFICER: Uh huh. She's a friend to the animals as well as a **philanthropist.**

ELLE: (*cross-examining a witness*) Isn't it the first **cardinal** rule of perm maintenance that you're forbidden to wet your hair for at least twenty-four hours after getting a perm at the risk of deactivating the ammonium thioglycolate?

CHUTNEY: Yes . . .

ELLE: And if, in fact, you weren't washing your hair as I suspect you weren't because your curls are still **intact,** wouldn't you have heard the gunshot . . . Which would mean that you would have had to have found Mrs. Windham with a gun in her hand to make your story **plausible,** isn't that right?

Movie: _____

Scenes: _____

Faux might mean _____

Philanthropist might mean _____

Cardinal might mean _____

Intact might mean _____

Plausible might mean _____

Hint: The choreographers of Elle's hilarious dance routine later became famous for the hit FOX television show *So You Think You Can Dance*.

Solutions

Let's see how you did. Check your answers and write the exact definitions. To help you memorize the vocabulary words, reread the movie excerpts or even act out the scenes with a friend.

Movie: *Legally Blonde,* Metro-Goldwyn-Mayer, 2001

Scenes: In the first excerpt, the Harvard admissions committee is considering Elle's (Reese Witherspoon) application to Harvard Law School. In the second excerpt, Elle is cross-examining a witness in her first trial.

Inside Scoop: Ali Larter, who you know as Niki Sanders from the TV show *Heroes*, plays the defendant in Elle's trial!

Faux means *fake. Faux* is French for *false.*

Philanthropist means *one who loves humans and donates money to help charities.* The word part *phil-* means *lover of,* and *anthrop-* means *humans.* Phil- helps you remember words such as *philosophy* (**love** of wisdom), *bibliophile* (one who **loves** books), *audiophile* (one who **loves** stereo equipment), and even *Philadelphia* (the city of brotherly **love**). *Anthrop-* helps you remember words such as *anthropocentrism* (the belief that **humans** are at the center of existence) and *anthropomorphism* (in literature, giving **human** qualities to nonhumans).

Cardinal means *main* or *critical.* Synonym: fundamental. *Cardinal* can also be used as a noun, in which case it refers to *a Roman Catholic dignitary, a bright red bird,* or *a deep red color.*

Intact means *complete or undamaged. Intact* actually breaks down to *in,* meaning *not,* and *tact-,* which refers to *touch.* So, *intact* means *not touched,* as in Chutney did not shower after getting her hair permed, so the curls are still **intact** (untouched, complete, undamaged). The word part *tact-* helps you remember **touch** words like *tactile* (relating to the sense of **touch**).

Plausible means *reasonable, probable, or believable.* Synonyms: credible, feasible.

Group 90

Here's an excerpt from a movie. See if you can name the movie, describe the scene, and define the boldface vocabulary words. Check your answers on the following page.

ELIZABETH: If an **adversary** demands **parley,** you can do them no harm until the parley is complete . . . I am here to **negotiate** the **cessation** of **hostilities** against Port Royal.

BARBOSSA: There are a lot of long words in there, Miss; we're **naught** but humble pirates. What is it that you want?

ELIZABETH: I want you to leave and never come back.

BARBOSSA: I'm **disinclined** to **acquiesce** to your request. Means "no."

ELIZABETH: Very well. I'll drop it. (*dangles medallion over the sea*)

BARBOSSA: Me holds are burstin' with **swag.** That bit of shine matters to us? Why?

Hint: "This is Aztec gold, one of 882 identical pieces they delivered in a stone chest to Cortés himself . . . But the greed of Cortés was **insatiable.**"

Movie: _____

Scene: _____

_____

Adversary might mean _____

Parley might mean _____

Negotiate might mean _____

Cessation might mean _____

Hostilities might mean _____

Naught might mean _____

Disinclined might mean _____

Acquiesce might mean_____

Swag might mean _____

Solutions

Let's see how you did. Check your answers and write the exact definitions. To help you memorize the vocabulary words, reread the movie excerpt or even act out the scene with a friend.

Movie: *Pirates of the Caribbean: The Curse of the Black Pearl,* Walt Disney Pictures, 2003

Scene: Elizabeth (Keira Knightley) has been captured by the pirate Barbossa (Geoffrey Rush) because she possesses the medallion that he and his crew need. She's got the heart of a pirate and doesn't give in easily.

Vocabulary in the Hint: *Insatiable* means *unable to be satisfied*. Synonyms: gluttonous, implacable, rapacious, ravenous, relentless, unappeasable, voracious.

Solutions (continued)

Adversary means *opponent*.

Parley means *conference between opposing sides in a dispute*. Of course, here it refers to the old pirate code, as set out by the pirates Morgan and Bartholomew, which grants the prisoner who declares *parley* temporary protection until she or he can have an audience with the enemy captain. The word *parliament* (assembly of lawmakers) comes from the same root as *parley*.

Negotiate means *discuss terms for*. Synonyms: arbitrate, compromise, conciliate, confer, debate, haggle, intercede, mediate, moderate, parley. *Negotiate* can also mean *find a way through,* as in the ship successfully **negotiated** the shallow waters.

Cessation means *end*. Synonym: termination.

Hostilities means *fighting* or *aggression*. Synonyms for *hostility*: belligerence, truculence.

Naught means *nothing*.

Disinclined means *unwilling*. Synonyms: averse, reluctant.

Acquiesce means *give in*. Synonyms: comply, oblige.

Swag means *loot, a pretty wreath of flowers,* or *an ornamental curtain*. I doubt that Captain Barbossa was bragging about his **flowers** or **curtains,** so he must have been referring to **loot!**

Quiz 9

I. Let's review some of the words that you've seen in Groups 81–90. Match each of the following words to the correct definition or synonym on the right. If you need help, refer back to the movie excerpts and definitions. Then check the solutions on page 238.

1. Unmitigated
2. Indifferent
3. Unfathomable
4. Pernicious
5. Agile
6. Utility
7. Iconoclast
8. Disparity
9. Tribute
10. Ominous
11. Pandering
12. Truncated
13. Rapacious
14. Cardinal
15. Plausible

A. Inscrutable
B. Nefarious
C. Apathetic
D. Curtailed
E. Categorical
F. Paean
G. Lithe
H. Efficacy
I. Credible
J. Avaricious
K. One who attacks cherished beliefs
L. Fundamental
M. Divergence
N. Obsequious
O. Menacing

II. Let's review several of the word parts that you've seen in Groups 81–90. Match each of the following word parts to the correct definition or synonym on the right. Then check the solutions on page 238.

16. Parity (as in *disparity*)
17. Dis- (as in *disparity*)
18. Phil- (as in *audiophile*)
19. Anthrop- (as in *anthropocentrism*)
20. Tact- (as in *tactile*)

A. Not
B. Humans
C. Touch
D. Equality
E. Lover of

III. Match each group of synonyms to its general meaning. Then check the solutions on page 238.

21. Absolute   A. Destructive or wicked
      Categorical
      Consummate
      Unconditional
      Unequivocal
      Unmitigated
      Unqualified
      Untempered

22. Baleful   B. Graceful
      Deleterious
      Inimical
      Insidious
      Maleficent
      Malevolent
      Malignant
      Nefarious
      Noxious
      Pernicious

23. Agile   C. Overly flattering or obedient
      Fleet-footed
      Limber
      Lithe
      Nimble
      Supple

24. Fawning   D. Complete
      Ingratiating
      Obsequious
      Oleaginous
      Pandering
      Servile
      Sycophantic
      Toady

Group 91

Here are two excerpts from a movie. See if you can name the movie, describe the scenes, and define the boldface vocabulary words. Check your answers on the following page.

Mary Jane: Tell me again. Was I really good? I was so nervous. My knees were shaking.

Peter: Your knees were fine.

Mary Jane: The applause wasn't very loud.

Peter: Yes, it was. Well, it's the **acoustics.** It's all about **diffusion.** It keeps the sound waves from grouping. You see when the sound waves, they **propagate**, then it's like an . . .

Mary Jane: You are such a nerd.

―――――――――

Dr. Connors: Don't let any of that get on you.

Peter: Why not?

Dr. Connors: It has the characteristics of a **symbiote,** which needs to bond to a host to survive. And sometimes these things in nature, when they bind, they can be hard to unbind.

Movie: _____

Scenes: _____

_____

Acoustics might mean _____

Diffusion might mean _____

Propagate might mean _____

Symbiote might mean _____

Hint: Remember what **arachna-** means?

Solutions

Let's see how you did. Check your answers and write the exact definitions. To help you memorize the vocabulary words, reread the movie excerpts or even act out the scenes with a friend.

Movie: *Spider-Man 3*, Columbia Pictures, 2007

Scenes: In the first excerpt, Peter (Tobey Maguire) tells Mary Jane (Kirsten Dunst) how great her Broadway performance was, and in the second excerpt, Peter's Columbia University physics professor, Dr. Connors (Dylan Baker), examines the symbiote.

Inside Scoop: Kirsten Dunst is a natural blonde and plays redhead Mary Jane, while Bryce Dallas Howard is a natural redhead and plays blonde Gwen Stacy. You might recognize Bryce and her signature red hair from her role as vengeful, redheaded vampire Victoria in *The Twilight Saga: Eclipse*. She took over the role from Rachelle Lefevre who had played Victoria in the *Twilight* and *New Moon* movies.

Vocabulary in the Hint: You learned from *My Big Fat Greek Wedding* (Group 9) and *Harry Potter and the Half-Blood Prince* (Group 82) that *arachna-* means *spider,* as in *arachnophobia* (fear of spiders).

Acoustics in this case means *the structure of a space that effects the transmission of sound. Acoustic* can also mean *related to sound or the sense of hearing.*

Diffusion means *spreading* and comes from *diffuse* (spread). *Diffuse* can also mean *wordy,* which brings up a great chance to review synonyms for *wordy:* circumlocutory, digressive, discursive, effusive, garrulous, loquacious, periphrastic, prolix, and verbose. You first learned all of these words in Group 2 (*Harry Potter and the Goblet of Fire*).

Propagate means *spread.* Synonyms: breed, disseminate, proliferate, promulgate.

Symbiote refers, in this movie, to *an alien being that bonds to another being in order to survive. Symbiote* comes from the word *symbiotic,* meaning *mutually beneficial. Sym-* means *together,* as in *symmetrical* (measured **together**— evenly proportioned) and *sympathy* (feeling **together**—compassion), and *bio-* means *life,* so *symbiotic* means *life together—mutually beneficial.*

Group 92

Here are three excerpts from a movie. See if you can name the movie, describe the scenes, and define the boldface vocabulary words. Check your answers on the following pages.

SISTER: Chris measured himself and those around him by a fiercely **rigorous** moral code. He risked what could have been a **relentlessly** lonely path, but found company in the characters of the books he loved . . . It was **inevitable** that Chris would break away, and when he did, he would do it with characteristic **immoderation.**

CHRISTOPHER: Two years he walks the Earth. No phone, no pool, no pets, no cigarettes. Ultimate freedom. An extremist. An **aesthetic** voyager whose home is the road. Escaped from Atlanta. Thou shalt not return, 'cause "the West is the best." And now after two rambling years comes the final and greatest adventure. The climactic battle to kill the false being within and victoriously conclude the spiritual **pilgrimage** . . . No longer to be poisoned by civilization, he flees and walks alone upon the land to become lost in the wild.

CHRISTOPHER: It should not be denied that being **footloose** has always exhilarated us. It is associated in our minds with escape from history and **oppression** and law and **irksome** obligations. Absolute freedom. And the road has always led west.

Movie: _____

Scenes: _____

_____

Hint: This film stars Emile Hirsch and has a surprising *cameo* (small role) by *The Hangover*'s Zach Galifianakis. It also feature's *Twilight*'s Kristen Stewart.

Group 92 (continued)

Rigorous might mean _____

_____

Relentlessly might mean _____

_____

Inevitable might mean _____

_____

Immoderation might mean _____

_____

Aesthetic might mean _____

_____

Pilgrimage might mean _____

_____

Footloose might mean _____

_____

Oppression might mean _____

_____

Irksome might mean _____

_____

Solutions

Let's see how you did. Check your answers and write the exact definitions. To help you memorize the vocabulary words, reread the movie excerpts or even act out the scenes with a friend.

Movie: *Into the Wild,* Paramount Vantage, 2007

Scenes: Christopher McCandless (Emile Hirsch) and his sister (Jena Malone) narrate his journey north into the Alaskan wilderness.

Rigorous means *thorough, strict,* or *demanding.* Synonyms: assiduous, conscientious, diligent, draconian, intransigent, meticulous, persnickety, punctilious, scrupulous, sedulous, stringent.

Relentlessly means *constantly* or *tirelessly.* Synonyms: incessantly, inexorably, interminably, unremittingly.

Inevitable means *unavoidable.* Synonyms: fated, ineluctable, ineludible, inexorable, predestined, predetermined

Immoderation means *excessiveness. Im-* means *not* or *lack of,* and *moderation* means *restraint,* so *immoderation* means *lack of restraint—excessiveness.* Synonym: intemperance.

Aesthetic means *concerned with true beauty.*

Pilgrimage means *religious or spiritual journey.*

Footloose means *free of commitments and able to travel,* as in "footloose and fancy-free," and as in the title of the film *Footloose,* which is about a teenager who **frees** a town from its strict restrictions on dancing. You can see the double meaning of that title, as the teen also gets the townspeople's feet moving—**foot**loose!

Oppression means *cruel and unfair treatment.* Synonyms: despotism, persecution, repression, subjection, subjugation, suppression, tyranny. Antonym: freedom.

Irksome means *annoying.* Synonyms: exasperating, galling, nettlesome, vexing.

Group 93

Here's an excerpt from a movie. See if you can name the movie, describe the scene, and define the boldface vocabulary words. Check your answers on the following page.

NARRATOR: A Lost World in South America, lurking in the shadow of **majestic** Paradise Falls, it sports plants and animals undiscovered by science. Who would dare set foot on this **inhospitable summit?** Why, our subject today, Charles Muntz! The **beloved** explorer lands his **dirigible,** *The Spirit of Adventure,* into Hampshire this week, completing a yearlong **expedition** to the Lost World.

Movie: _____

Scene: _____

_____

Majestic might mean _____

Inhospitable might mean _____

Summit might mean _____

Beloved might mean _____

Dirigible might mean _____

Expedition might mean _____

Hint: "You ever heard of a snipe? Bird. Beady eyes. Every night it sneaks in my yard and gobbles my poor azaleas. I'm elderly and **infirm;** I can't catch it. If only someone could help me."

Solutions

Let's see how you did. Check your answers and write the exact definitions. To help you memorize the vocabulary words, reread the movie excerpt or even act out the scene with a friend.

Movie: *Up,* Walt Disney Pictures, 2009

Scene: At the beginning of the film, young Carl Fredricksen is watching a movie about his idol, explorer Charles Muntz (voiced by Christopher Plummer), and his expedition to Paradise Falls in South America.

Vocabulary in the Hint: *Infirm* means *weak.* Synonyms: debilitated, decrepit, feeble, frail.

Majestic means *beautiful* or *dignified.* Synonyms: august, distinguished, noble, resplendent, stately, sumptuous.

Inhospitable means *harsh and unwelcoming.* Synonyms: austere, bleak, desolate, inimical, spartan, stark.

Summit means *highest point.* Synonyms: acme, apex, apogee, peak, pinnacle, zenith. (A fancy word for the *lowest point* is *nadir.*) At the beginning of the first *Iron Man* movie, Tony Stark is receiving the fictitious **Apogee** Award for excellence. The word *summit* and its synonyms, including **apogee,** are often used in the name of awards that honor the **highest point** of achievement in a field or pursuit.

Beloved looks like "be loved" and means exactly that, *deeply loved.*

Dirigible refers to an *airship, such as a blimp or zeppelin, that has a balloon or huge container that is filled with a gas that makes the ship lighter than air and able to fly.*

Expedition means *journey with a purpose.*

Here are four excerpts from a movie. See if you can name the movie, describe the scenes, and define the boldface vocabulary words. Check your answers on the following pages.

NELL: While **archetypal** outsiders such as myself rarely fit comfortably into high school environments, *this* is as good as your life will get. The big football star and his **vacuous** cheerleader girlfriend . . . fast forward a few years . . . your little wife . . . is . . . indulging in **squalid** sexual encounters with your friends behind your back.

TEACHER: I know who J. Lo is, Nell. I'm just very interested to hear what you perceive qualifies her for such a unique **accolade.**

NELL: Right. Well the thing about J. Lo is that she's from the streets. And now she's like this big movie star, and she's still really cool. She used to have a little, now she has a lot, but she's still Jenny from the block, and I think that's pretty damn great . . .

WOODY: Woody Dean, you are an idiot and a **philistine.**

WOODY: "Shall I compare thee to a summer's day? Thou art more lovely and more **temperate:** Rough winds do shake the darling buds of May . . . "

WOODY: Think about it, Harry. Are you willing to betray the love of a good woman for the cheap thrill of a **tawdry** one-night stand?

Movie: _____

Scenes: _____

_____

Hint: Kinda like *17 Again,* but different, and with Kevin Zegers instead of Zac Efron.

Archetypal might mean _____

_____

Vacuous might mean _____

_____

Squalid might mean _____

_____

Accolade might mean _____

_____

Philistine might mean _____

_____

Temperate might mean _____

_____

Tawdry might mean _____

_____

Solutions

Let's see how you did. Check your answers and write the exact definitions. To help you memorize the vocabulary words, reread the movie excerpts or even act out the scenes with a friend.

Movie: *It's a Boy Girl Thing,* Icon Entertainment, 2006

Scenes: In the first excerpt, Nell (Samaire Armstrong) tells off Woody (Kevin Zegers) after he and his buddy intentionally *douse* (drench) her with water. In the second excerpt, Nell and Woody have switched bodies, and Nell is pissed that Woody made a fool of her in class. In the third, Woody and Nell are studying for Nell's Yale admissions interview, and in the last excerpt, Woody tries to talk Harry out of cheating on his girlfriend.

Inside Scoop: Woody's mom is played by Sharon Osbourne, Ozzy Osbourne's wife.

Solutions (continued)

Archetypal means *typical*. Synonyms: exemplary, prototypical, quintessential, stereotypical.

Vacuous means *mindless or empty*, like a *vacuum* (totally empty space) in science class. Synonyms: fatuous, inane, insipid, vacant, vapid. Antonym: intelligent. You might remember this word from *Zoolander*—after Mugatu (Will Ferrell) declares his need for a "dumb, **vacuous** moron," you are introduced to veteran model Derek Zoolander, three-time Male Model of the Year.

Squalid means *dirty* or *immoral*. Synonyms: sordid, tawdry.

Accolade means *honor*. Synonyms: kudos, plaudits, tribute.

Philistine means *a person hostile to or ignorant of the arts and intellectual pursuits*.

Temperate means *mild*. Synonym: clement. This is the second time in this book that you've seen this Shakespearean sonnet, which begins, "Shall I compare thee to a summer's day?" Do you remember the other place? Answer: *Clueless* (Group 16).

Tawdry means *tasteless, vulgar,* or *immoral*. Synonyms: garish, gaudy.

Group 95

Here are three excerpts from a movie. See if you can name the movie, describe the scenes, and define the boldface vocabulary words. Check your answers on the following page.

HARRY: And how long have you been in love with Karl, our **enigmatic** chief designer?

SARAH: Um, two years, seven months, three days and I suppose an hour and thirty minutes . . .

HARRY: I just thought maybe the time had come to do something about it.

SARAH: Like what?

HARRY: Invite him out for a drink and then . . . casually drop into the conversation the fact that you'd like to marry him . . .

———————

SAM: She doesn't even know my name, and even if she did, she'd **despise** me. She's the coolest girl in school. And everyone worships her because she's heaven.

———————

JOE: You're supposed to be at Elton John's . . .

BILLY: I was there for a minute or two and then I had an **epiphany** . . . It was about Christmas . . . I realized that Christmas is the time to be with the people you love. And much as it grieves me to say it, it might be that the people I love is, in fact, you.

Movie: _____

Scenes: _____

Enigmatic might mean _____

Despise might mean _____

Epiphany might mean _____

Hint: This film stars nearly every British movie star.

Solutions

Let's see how you did. Check your answers and write the exact definitions. To help you memorize the vocabulary words, reread the movie excerpts or even act out the scenes with a friend.

Movie: *Love Actually,* Universal Pictures, 2003

Scenes: In the first excerpt, Harry (Alan Rickman) is encouraging Sarah (Laura Linney) to ask out Karl. In the second excerpt, Sam is telling his stepfather (Liam Neeson) about his crush on a girl at school, and in the third excerpt, Billy (Bill Nighy) realizes that he loves Joe.

Inside Scoop: Sarah's love interest Karl (Rodrigo Santoro) is none other than *Lost's* Paulo and *300's* King Xerxes!

Enigmatic means *mysterious* or *difficult to understand*. Synonyms: abstruse, arcane, impenetrable, inscrutable, recondite. Standardized tests love to use these words, so write them five times to help you to memorize them.

Despise means *hate*. Synonyms: abhor, detest, disdain, loathe, scorn.

Epiphany means *sudden realization of great truth*. Synonym: revelation.

Group 96

Here are two excerpts from a movie. See if you can name the movie, describe the scenes, and define the boldface vocabulary words. Check your answers on the following page.

JESSICA: I don't know why you want to sit through all those zombies eating people, and no hot guys kissing anybody. It's gross. Like, why are there that many zombie movies anyway? . . . Is it supposed to be a **metaphor** for **consumerism?** 'Cause don't be so pleased with your own, like, self-**reverential** cleverness. You know?

_____

ARO: Remarkable! She **confounds** us all. So what do we do with you now?

MARCUS: You already know what you're going to do, Aro.

CAIUS: She knows too much. She's a **liability.**

ARO: That's true. Felix . . .

Movie: _____

Scenes: _____

_____

Metaphor might mean _____

Consumerism might mean _____

Reverential might mean _____

Confounds might mean _____

Liability might mean _____

Hint: This film premiered on November 16, 2009, the night of a crescent moon.

Solutions

Let's see how you did. Check your answers and write the exact definitions. To help you memorize the vocabulary words, reread the movie excerpts or even act out the scenes with a friend.

Movie: *The Twilight Saga: New Moon,* Summit Entertainment, 2009

Scenes: In the first excerpt, Jessica (Anna Kendrick) and Bella (Kristen Stewart) have just been to a movie that Bella chose, so it was a gory, grotesque, romance-free zombie film. In the second excerpt, Bella, Alice (Ashley Greene), and Edward are meeting with the Volturi (a group of very old vampires who enforce vampire law).

Metaphor means *comparison.* For the SAT Subject Test in Literature, you need to know two kinds of comparisons, metaphor and simile. *Metaphor is when two things are compared,* and *simile is when two things are compared using the words* **like** *or* **as.** So, "Edward the sparkler" is a metaphor, and "Jacob is **like** a big, huggable teddy bear" is a simile.

Consumerism refers to *society's obsession with buying stuff. Consume* means *eat, use, buy,* or *destroy* and *-ism* can mean *philosophy,* so *consumerism* is the *philosophy of eating, using, or buying stuff,* which some say is *destroy*ing the planet. Here are two other isms: *hedonism* (philosophy that advocates seeking pleasure) and *existentialism* (belief that individuals must find their *own* meaning to existence).

Reverential means *with deep respect,* so *self-reverential* means *with deep respect for oneself.* But Jessica means it in a *pejorative* (critical) way, referring to someone who is arrogant, with too much ego about his or her own cleverness.

Confounds means *stumps* and makes me think of the Confundus charm in the *Harry Potter* books and movies that **confuses** the victim. Hermione used this charm on Cormac McLaggen during Quidditch tryouts in *Harry Potter and the Half-Blood Prince.* Synonyms: baffles, mystifies, perplexes. Aro is **baffled** that Jane's power does not work on Bella.

Liability means *problem* or *debt.* The opposite of *liability* is *asset* (a *resource* or *help,* rather than a *problem*). Asset and liability are accounting words . . . and you thought accounting couldn't be sexy.

Group 97

Here's an excerpt from a movie. See if you can name the movie, describe the scene, and define the boldface vocabulary words. Check your answers on the following page.

S.: We're from the Union. We represent the workers in all magical industries, both evil and **benign**. Are you feeling at all **degraded** or **repressed**?

Movie: _____

Scene: _____

_____

Benign might mean _____

_____

Degraded might mean _____

_____

Repressed might mean _____

_____

Hint: Think green.

Solutions

Let's see how you did. Check your answers and write the exact definitions. To help you memorize the vocabulary words, reread the movie excerpt or even act out the scene with a friend.

Movie: *Shrek 2*, DreamWorks, 2004

Scene: Shrek, Donkey, and Puss in Boots sneak into Fairy Godmother's potion factory by pretending to be inspectors from the Union.

Benign means *kind* or *harmless,* the opposite of *evil* or *harmful.* Synonyms: innocuous, nonmalignant. You hear these words a lot on doctor shows such as *House, Grey's Anatomy,* and *Scrubs*—a *benign* tumor is *harmless,* and a *malignant* tumor is *cancerous* (*malignant* means *harmful*).

Degraded in this case means *disrespected.* It can also mean *deteriorated.* Synonyms: demeaned, denigrated.

Repressed means *put down* or *subdued.* Synonyms: oppressed, subjugated, tyrannized.

Here are four excerpts from a movie. See if you can name the movie, describe the scenes, and define the boldface vocabulary words. Check your answers on the following page.

SEBASTIAN: And then Escobar comes in and says . . . , "I read your piece on Gaddafi, and I think you captured his **narcissism** perfectly."

JOHN: No, don't worry. That was like, uh, . . . it sounds so awkward now, like I just had this, like, very idiotic **soliloquy** that doesn't apply . . .

ARNIE: Get her a gift. That will **dissipate** some of the anger . . .

JOHN: That's thoughtful. It's a good idea. In fact, maybe I'll get on it right now.

JOHN: . . . we got a lot of cranks in Broward County . . .

ARNIE: Yeah, but what I'm trying to say, with all due respect, is that you are one of them . . .

JOHN: Everyone wants to think, oh, he's turning forty, he's become a **curmudgeon.**

Movie: _____

Scenes: _____

Narcissism might mean _____

Soliloquy might mean _____

Dissipate might mean _____

Curmudgeon might mean _____

Hint: "A dog doesn't care if you're rich or poor, clever or dull, smart or dumb. Give him your heart, and he'll give you his."

Solutions

Let's see how you did. Check your answers and write the exact definitions. To help you memorize the vocabulary words, reread the movie excerpts or even act out the scenes with a friend.

Movie: *Marley & Me,* 20th Century Fox, 2008

Scenes: In the first excerpt, Sebastian (Eric Dane) is describing his experience interviewing Colombian drug lord Pablo Escobar. In the second excerpt, John (Owen Wilson) has just come home and told his wife, Jenny (Jennifer Anniston), that maybe they're not ready to have a baby, but Jenny cuts him off to say, "John, I'm pregnant." In the third excerpt, John's boss, Arnie (Alan Arkin), recommends that John buy Jenny a gift. John buys a beautiful necklace, and when Jenny opens it, she immediately loves it. But while she thanks and kisses John, Marley (their dog) snatches the necklace, runs away, and eats it. John winds up having to hose down Marley's poop to fish it out. In the fourth excerpt, John's boss points out that John has been grumpy (curmudgeonly) lately.

Narcissism means *egotism* and comes from the name Narcissus, a mythological hunter who fell in love with his own reflection in a pond. Synonyms: solipsism, vanity.

Soliloquy means *speech where one thinks aloud, often alone.* Synonyms: aside, monologue. *Soliloquy* comes from *solo-* meaning *alone* and *loq-* meaning *speak,* so *speaking alone. Loq-* helps you remember high-level words such as *colloquial* (informal **speaking**), *grandiloquence* (pompous **speaking**), and *loquacious* (**speaking** a lot).

Dissipate means *dissolve* or *evaporate.* Synonym: evanesce. You learned *evanesce* from Briony's story of Arabella in *Atonement* (Group 74).

Curmudgeon means *grouch.* I've seen this word frequently on standardized tests, and now you know it thanks to *Marley & Me!*

Grup 99

Here are three excerpts from a movie. See if you can name the movie, describe the scenes, and define the boldface vocabulary words. Check your answers on the following page.

CARRIE: With my mind **prenuptially** preoccupied, I became **delinquent** with my library books. So, now the tragic love stories of *Wuthering Heights* and *Love Story* were going to cost me more than a few tears.

_____

CARRIE: Louise, now I may not get texts, I may not send texts, but trust me, the **subtext** of that text: bootie!

_____

CARRIE: Some love stories aren't **epic** novels. Some are short stories, but that doesn't make them any less filled with love.

Movie: _____

Scenes: _____

_____

Prenuptially might mean _____

_____

Delinquent might mean _____

_____

Subtext might mean _____

_____

Epic might mean _____

_____

Hint: Carrie, Samantha, Charlotte, and Miranda

Solutions

Let's see how you did. Check your answers and write the exact definitions. To help you memorize the vocabulary words, reread the movie excerpts or even act out the scenes with a friend.

Movie: *Sex and the City,* New Line Cinema, 2008

Scenes: In the first excerpt, Carrie (Sarah Jessica Parker) realizes that the New York Public Library is her perfect wedding venue. In the second excerpt, she is out for drinks with her assistant, Louise (Jennifer Hudson), and in the third excerpt, Carrie narrates as Samantha (Kim Cattrall) breaks up with Smith (Jason Lewis).

Inside Scoop: The director of the film had to beg the Smithsonian Museum in Washington, D.C., to loan out Carrie's desk, which had been donated after the television series ended.

Prenuptially means *before marriage. Pre-* means *before* and *nuptial* refers to *marriage.*

Delinquent means *overdue* or *criminal.* Synonyms: derelict, errant, remiss.

Subtext means *underlying theme or message. Sub-* means *under,* as in *subterranean* (*terra-* means *earth,* so *under earth—underground*).

Epic means *grand* or *monumental,* as in Homer's **epic** poems, which are long and **monumental.**

Group 100

Here are three excerpts from a movie. See if you can name the movie, describe the scenes, and define the boldface vocabulary words. Check your answers on the following pages.

DENISE: **Ambulatory** is to mobile as fruitful is to: **Nefarious, Fertile, Munificent,** or **Penurious?**

BETH: Fertile!

DENISE: Good. OK, Dakota . . . **Intrepid** is to valorous as **multitudinous** is to: **Prostrate, Flagrant, Plethoric,** or Static?

DAKOTA: Are you speaking English?

TERRY: Come on. Try it.

DAKOTA: I don't know any of those words.

BETH: OK. Well, just think of their relation to each other. Intrepid is to valorous as multitudinous is to . . .

DAKOTA: "B."

DENISE: No, sorry. It's "C."

_____

BETH: **Enigmatic** is to **inscrutable** as **surreptitious** is to . . .

_____

BETH: Aristocrat is to **imperious** as **supplicant** is to: Cowardly, Awkward, **Servile,** or Arrogant?

Movie: _____

Scenes: _____

_____

Hint: The name of the movie contains one of the girls' names from the dialogue.

Ambulatory might mean _____

Nefarious might mean _____

Munificent might mean _____

Penurious might mean _____

Intrepid might mean _____

Multitudinous might mean _____

Prostrate might mean _____

Flagrant might mean _____

Plethoric might mean _____

Enigmatic might mean _____

Inscrutable might mean _____

Surreptitious might mean _____

Imperious might mean _____

Supplicant might mean _____

Servile might mean _____

Solutions

Let's see how you did. Check your answers and write the exact definitions. To help you memorize the vocabulary words, reread the movie excerpts or even act out the scenes with a friend.

Movie: *Dakota Skye,* Desert Skye Entertainment, 2008

Scenes: In these three excerpts, Dakota (Eileen Boylan) is studying for the SAT with her friends. You may not have seen this movie, but you should; it's a touching love story about a high school student who can sense the truth, even when people lie, and it has a ton of excellent vocabulary words in it!

Solutions (continued)

Ambulatory means *able to walk or move*. *Ambl-* implies *walk,* as in *ambulate* (walk around) and *amble* (stroll).

Nefarious means *wicked*. Synonyms: baleful, depraved, heinous, impious, iniquitous, malevolent, pernicious.

Munificent means *very generous*. Synonyms: beneficent, bounteous, bountiful, magnanimous, openhanded.

Penurious can mean *poor* or *miserly*. Synonym: parsimonious.

Intrepid means *fearless*.

Multitudinous means *numerous*. Synonyms: abundant, copious, multifarious, myriad, profuse, prolific.

Prostrate means *lying face down on the ground*.

Flagrant means *obvious*. Synonym: blatant.

Plethoric means *excessive*.

Enigmatic means *mysterious*. Synonyms: abstruse, arcane, impenetrable, inscrutable, recondite.

Inscrutable means *difficult to understand*. Synonyms: abstruse, arcane, enigmatic, impenetrable, recondite.

Surreptitious means *secret*. Synonyms: clandestine, covert, furtive.

Imperious means *bossy, controlling, or domineering*. Synonym: peremptory.

Supplicant means *one who prays*.

Servile means *overly obedient*. Synonyms: obsequious, sycophantic, today.

Quiz 10

I. Let's review some of the words that you've seen in Groups 91–100. Match each of the following words to the correct definition or synonym on the right. If you need help, refer back to the movie excerpts and definitions. Then check the solutions on page 238.

1. Propagate
2. Symbiotic
3. Summit
4. Accolade
5. Tawdry
6. Enigmatic
7. Despise
8. Benign
9. Dissipate
10. Curmudgeon
11. Delinquent
12. Ambulatory
13. Munificent
14. Penurious
15. Imperious

A. Plaudits
B. Apogee
C. Proliferate
D. Abstruse
E. Mutually beneficial
F. Grouch
G. Garish
H. Loathe
I. Able to move
J. Innocuous
K. Peremptory
L. Parsimonious
M. Magnanimous
N. Evanesce
O. Derelict

II. Let's review several of the word parts that you've seen in Groups 91–100. Match each of the following word parts to the correct definition or synonym on the right. Then check the solutions on page 238.

16. Sym- (as in *symbiotic*)
17. Loq- (as in *loquacious*)
18. Solo- (as in *soliloquy*)
19. Pre- (as in *prenuptial*)
20. Sub- (as in *subterranean*)
21. Ambl- (as in *amble*)

A. Before
B. Under
C. Walk
D. Together
E. Alone
F. Speak

III. Match each group of synonyms to its general meaning. Then check the solutions on page 238.

22. Accolade
    Kudos
    Plaudits
    Tribute

    A. Numerous

23. Abhor
    Despise
    Detest
    Disdain
    Loathe
    Scorn

    B. Secret

24. Beneficent
    Bounteous
    Bountiful
    Magnanimous
    Munificent
    Openhanded

    C. Honor

25. Abundant
    Copious
    Multifarious
    Multitudinous
    Myriad
    Profuse
    Prolific

    D. Generous

26. Clandestine
    Covert
    Furtive
    Surreptitious

    E. Hate

27. Obsequious
    Servile
    Sycophantic

    F. Excessively flattering or
       obedient

Quiz Solutions

Quiz 1	Quiz 2	Quiz 3	Quiz 4	Quiz 5
1. E	1. E	1. D	1. D	1. C
2. A	2. F	2. A	2. E	2. F
3. F	3. A	3. F	3. B	3. A
4. B	4. B	4. B	4. G	4. G
5. H	5. H	5. C	5. A	5. B
6. C	6. C	6. I	6. C	6. H
7. D	7. D	7. J	7. L	7. E
8. M	8. J	8. E	8. J	8. J
9. J	9. K	9. N	9. K	9. K
10. I	10. G	10. G	10. N	10. D
11. N	11. I	11. O	11. F	11. N
12. G	12. O	12. H	12. I	12. M
13. K	13. N	13. M	13. O	13. I
14. O	14. L	14. K	14. H	14. O
15. L	15. M	15. L	15. M	15. L
16. C	16. D	16. E	16. C	16. D
17. A	17. E	17. F	17. A	17. C
18. F	18. A	18. D	18. E	18. E
19. E	19. B	19. C	19. B	19. A
20. B	20. C	20. A	20. D	20. B
21. D	21. E	21. B	21. B	21. C
22. D	22. A	22. C	22. D	22. E
23. A	23. B	23. A	23. E	23. A
24. E	24. C	24. D	24. A	24. B
25. B	25. D	25. B	25. C	25. D
26. C				

Quiz Solutions (continued)

Quiz 6	Quiz 7	Quiz 8	Quiz 9	Quiz 10
1. E	1. D	1. C	1. E	1. C
2. C	2. C	2. D	2. C	2. E
3. A	3. A	3. A	3. A	3. B
4. F	4. F	4. F	4. B	4. A
5. I	5. B	5. B	5. G	5. G
6. B	6. H	6. E	6. H	6. D
7. H	7. E	7. J	7. K	7. H
8. D	8. J	8. K	8. M	8. J
9. L	9. G	9. G	9. F	9. N
10. N	10. L	10. L	10. O	10. F
11. G	11. M	11. H	11. N	11. O
12. J	12. O	12. O	12. D	12. I
13. M	13. N	13. I	13. J	13. M
14. O	14. K	14. M	14. L	14. L
15. K	15. I	15. N	15. I	15. K
16. D	16. C	16. E	16. D	16. D
17. E	17. B	17. A	17. A	17. F
18. B	18. E	18. B	18. E	18. E
19. A	19. A	19. C	19. B	19. A
20. C	20. D	20. D	20. C	20. B
21. C	21. D	21. C	21. D	21. C
22. A	22. A	22. A	22. A	22. C
23. E	23. B	23. B	23. B	23. E
24. B	24. F	24. D	24. C	24. D
25. F	25. C			25. A
26. D	26. E			26. B
				27. F

Glossary

Abdicate give up one's office. Synonyms: *abjure, cede, demit, disclaim, forsake, relinquish, renounce, repudiate, resign, retire, vacate*

Abide tolerate or obey

Absolutely completely. Synonyms: *unconditionally, unmitigatedly, unqualifiedly*

Absolution forgiveness. Synonyms: *acquittal, clemency, dispensation, exculpation, exoneration, indulgence, shrift.* Antonym: *condemnation*

Abstract theoretical rather than actual

Abyss a deep gorge or ravine. Synonym: *chasm*

Accessory add-on, someone who assists a criminal in committing a crime. Synonyms: *adjunct, adornment, appendage, appurtenance, embellishment, frill, trimming*

Accolade honor. Synonyms: *kudos, plaudits, tribute*

Acoustics the structure of a space that effects the transmission of sound; related to sound or the sense of hearing

Acquiesce give in. Synonyms: *comply, oblige*

Acutest severest. Synonyms for acute: *dire, drastic, dreadful, grave*

Adage a saying, or a short and memorable statement of truth. Synonyms: *aphorism, apothegm, axiom, dictum, epigram, maxim, precept, proverb, saw, truism*

Adversary opponent

Aerophobia fear of flying

Aesthetic concerned with true beauty

Affect influence or have an effect on

Affiliates individuals joined as a group

Aggressor the one who attacks first. Synonyms: *assailant, instigator*

Agile able to move quickly. Synonyms: *fleet-footed, limber, lithe, nimble, supple*

Alacrity eagerness. Synonyms: *ardor, avidity, dispatch, fervor, keenness*

Alight land

Alliteration the literary device of using the same consonant sound at the beginning of successive words

Altruistic selfless. Synonyms: *beneficent, benevolent, bounteous, charitable, humanitarian, munificent, philanthropic*

Amble stroll

Ambulate walk around

Ambulatory able to walk or move

Amenable willing or open. Synonyms: *acquiescent, compliant, obliging*

Amiable friendly and pleasant. Synonyms: *affable, amicable, convivial, cordial, genial, gregarious, simpatico*

Anarchy disorder. Synonyms: *bedlam, chaos, mayhem, pandemonium, turmoil*

Angst struggle or face discomfort; anxiety or uneasiness. Synonyms: *disquietude, trepidation*

Anguish extreme pain. Synonyms: *agony, desolation, despair, despondency, wretchedness*

Anthropocentrism the belief that humans are at the center of existence

Anthropomorphism in literature, giving human qualities to nonhumans

Apiary a place where bees are kept

Arachnids spiders, scorpions, mites, and ticks

Arachnophobia fear of spiders

Archaic outdated. Synonyms: *anachronistic, antediluvian, antiquated, bygone, defunct, démodé, extinct, obsolete, outmoded, passé*

Archetypal typical. Synonyms: *exemplary, prototypical, quintessential, stereotypical*

Ardently eagerly or passionately. Synonyms: *avidly, fervently, keenly, zealously*

Aria solo from an opera

Aristocracy the upper class or nobility

Articulate well-spoken

Asset a resource or help. Antonym: *liability*

Assuage soothe or satisfy. Synonyms: *allay, alleviate, ameliorate, conciliate, mollify, pacify, palliate, placate*

Astute intelligent and insightful. Synonyms: *canny, incisive, judicious, keen, perspicacious, sagacious, savvy, shrewd, wise*

Atheist a person who believes that there is no God

Atonement the act of making up for a sin or bad deed

Audiophile one who loves stereo equipment

Auspicious likely to bring good fortune. Synonyms: *felicitous, opportune, propitious, providential*

Aviary a place where birds are kept

Avuncular of an uncle

Belligerent hostile. Synonyms: *bellicose, inimical, pugnacious, truculent*

Beloved deeply loved

Benign kind or harmless. Synonyms: *innocuous, nonmalignant*

Bereavement grief from the loss of a loved one

Bestride extend across or straddle

Bibliophile one who loves books

Blithely with insensitive cheerfulness and lack of concern

Bonanza good fortune, jackpot

Bon appétit French word that translates to "enjoy the meal"

Bonhomie good nature or friendliness

Bonny good looking

Bough tree branch

Bourgeois the conventional and materialistic middle class. Synonym: *provincial*

Brio spirit. Synonyms: *gusto, verve, vigor, vivacity, zest*

Camouflage disguise. Synonyms: *facade, pretense*

Candor honesty. Synonyms: *bluntness, forthrightness, frankness*

Capitalist relating to the profit-based economic system in which resources are privately owned

Caprice sudden change of mood or behavior

Capricious changing too quickly or easily. Synonyms: *erratic, fickle, fluctuating, impulsive, inconstant, labile, mercurial, mutable, protean, temperamental, volatile, whimsical.* Antonym: *stable*

Cardinal main, critical, a Roman Catholic dignitary, a bright red bird, a deep red color. Synonym: *fundamental*

Carnage slaughter. Synonym: *massacre*

Carnivorous flesh-eating

Cast aspersions on insultingly criticize. Synonyms: *belittle, decry, defame, denigrate, denounce, disparage, impugn, libel, malign, pillory, slander, vilify*

Cavalier unconcerned or overly casual. Synonyms: *dismissive, flippant, indifferent, insouciant, offhand*

Censor to edit the contents of

Censure harsh and official criticism. Synonyms: *admonishment, castigation, condemnation, excoriation, obloquy, opprobrium, rebuke, reprimand, reproach, reproof, vituperation*

Cerulean sky blue. Synonym: *azure*

Cessation end. Synonym: *termination*

Chalice cup or goblet

Chaotic disordered. Synonyms: *anarchic, in pandemonium, in turmoil*

Charismatic charming

Chasm deep crack or gap. Synonyms: *abyss, breach, cleft, crevasse, crevice, fault, fissure, fracture, rift, rupture, schism*

Chaste nonsexual

Clad clothed

Clemency mercy. Synonyms: *forbearance, leniency*

Colloquial informal speaking

Colossal very large

Colossus something or someone extremely large or important

Conditional not complete

Conflagration fire

Confounds stumps. Synonyms: *baffles, mystifies, perplexes*

Congeniality friendliness and pleasantness. Synonyms: *amiability, amity, conviviality, geniality, hospitality*

Connotation implication

Consequences negative results. Synonyms: *aftermath, ramifications, repercussions*

Consolations sympathy, comfort. Synonyms: *condolences, solace*

Consumerism society's obsession with buying stuff

Contrite regretful for wrongdoing. Synonyms: *penitent, remorseful, repentant*

Convictions firmly held beliefs, a jury's pronouncement of guilt. Synonym: *certitude*

Cornucopia abundance. Synonyms: *bounty, profusion*

Cotillions formal parties

Credo declaration of beliefs. Synonyms: *axiom, canon, conviction, creed, doctrine, dogma, ideology, tenet*

Crimson purplish-red

Crucible place to test, change, or develop

Curmudgeon grouch

Cursory superficial and quick. Synonyms: *casual, desultory, fleeting, hasty, perfunctory*

Dauntless fearless. Synonyms: *audacious, doughty, indomitable, intrepid, plucky, resolute, spirited, valiant*

Debutante a young woman making her official first

appearance as a woman in high society

Decathlon contest of ten events

Decorum proper behavior. Synonyms: *conventions, etiquette, propriety, protocol, punctilio*

Degradation deterioration, humiliation. Synonym: *atrophy*

Degraded disrespected; deteriorated. Synonyms: *demeaned, denigrated*

Deign do something beneath one's dignity. Synonyms: *condescend, demean oneself, vouchsafe*

Delinquent overdue; criminal. Synonyms: *derelict, errant, remiss*

Delirium madness characterized by confused thinking, disrupted speech, and hallucinations. Synonyms: *dementia, derangement, hallucination, hysteria, incoherence*

Demeaning humiliating. Synonyms: *degrading, ignominious, inglorious*

Democracy government by the people

Demographic population of people

Deployed utilized, positioned

Depraved corrupt, wicked. Synonyms: *baleful, execrable, impious, iniquitous, malevolent, nefarious, pernicious, reprehensible, villainous*

Derision insulting ridicule. Synonyms: *contempt, denigration, disdain, disparagement, disrespect, insults, lampooning, satire, scorn*

Desperate miserable, extremely needy, or hopeless. Synonyms: *anguished, desolate, despairing, despondent, distraught, forlorn, wretched*

Despise hate. Synonyms: *abhor, detest, disdain, loathe, scorn*

Devastation destruction, agony. Synonyms: *anguish, annihilation, demolition, desolation, despoliation, havoc, ruination, wreckage*

Diatribe angry, attacking speech. Synonyms: *broadside, fulmination, harangue, invective, onslaught, philippic, polemic, rant, tirade*

Diffuse spread, wordy

Diffusion spreading

Dilettantes amateurs or people who take part in something in a casual and uncommitted way. Synonym: *dabblers*

Dirigible an airship, such as a blimp or zeppelin, that has a balloon or huge container that is filled with a gas that makes the ship lighter than air and able to fly

Disenfranchised disempowered

Disinclined unwilling. Synonyms: *averse, reluctant*

Disparity large difference. Synonyms: *discrepancy, divergence, gap, variance*

Dissipate dissolve, evaporate. Synonym: *evanesce*

Diversity variety. Synonyms: *array, heterogeneity, mélange, multifariousness, multiplicity, variegation*

Divine pertaining to God, noble, admirable

Dominant commanding

Draconian excessively harsh and severe, especially regarding enforcing laws

Dramatis personae participants

Eclectic from varied sources. Synonyms: *disparate, heterogeneous, manifold, motley, multifarious, myriad, sundry*

Effect bring about

Effulgence brightness, radiance, or showing energy and joy. Synonym: *ebullience*

Egregious shocking or terribly bad. Synonyms: *abhorrent, abominable, appalling, atrocious, dreadful, grievous, heinous, horrendous*

Elasticity springiness. Synonyms: *pliability, resilience, suppleness*

Elitist snobbishly favoring the wealthy or powerful

Elixir medicinal or magical potion

Embeds puts firmly in place

Emetophobia fear of vomiting

Enamored smitten

Engorged swollen. Synonyms: *distended, tumescent, tumid, turgid*

Engrossing absorbing or all-consuming

Enigmatic mysterious or difficult to understand. Synonyms: *abstruse, arcane, impenetrable, inscrutable, recondite*

Entitled having a right

Entrepreneurs self-employed business people

Epic grand or monumental

Epiphany sudden realization of great truth. Synonym: *revelation*

Era time period of history. Synonyms: *eon, epoch*

Eradicate erase completely. Synonym: *expunge*

Ergo therefore. Synonyms: *consequently, hence, whence*

Erratic inconsistent and unpredictable. Synonyms: *arbitrary, capricious, fickle, impetuous, mercurial, sporadic*

Eternity timelessness, forever

Etiquette proper or polite behavior. Synonyms: *decorum, propriety, protocol*

Evanesce disappear

Evanescent about to disappear. Synonyms: *ephemeral, fleeting, fugitive, transient, transitory.* Antonyms: *eternal, permanent*

Everlasting lasting forever

Execrable appalling. Synonyms: *abhorrent, abysmal, atrocious, deplorable, egregious, lamentable, loathsome, odious, reprehensible, vile*

Executive lawmaking or managerial

Exile banishment. Synonym: *expatriation*

Existential the belief that each person must find his or her own meaning to existence

Expedition journey with a purpose, speed. Synonym: *haste*

Expiation atonement

Extinct no longer existing

Extradition moving of a criminal or criminal suspect from one country to another. Synonyms: *deportation, expatriation, repatriation*

Extrinsic from outside

Farce mockery, slapstick comedy, or ridiculous situation

Farcical ridiculous. Synonyms: *absurd, ludicrous, nonsensical, preposterous, risible*

Fastidious very clean or very attentive to details. Synonyms: *assiduous, finicky, meticulous, punctilious, scrupulous, sedulous*

Faux fake

Fecund fertile

Fickle unpredictable or changing too easily. Synonyms: *capricious, erratic, impetuous, mercurial, vacillating, whimsical*

Fictitious not real

Filial of a son or daughter

Flagrant obvious. Synonym: *blatant*

Fleeting disappearing or passing quickly. Synonyms: *ephemeral, evanescent, fugitive, impermanent, transient, transitory*

Follies foolishness. Synonyms: *imprudence, indiscretion, injudiciousness, rashness, recklessness*

Footloose free of commitments and able to travel

Fortuitous lucky

Franchise given the right to vote

Frivolity lightheartedness. Synonyms: *gaiety, glee, jocularity, jollity, joviality, levity, merriment, mirth.* Antonyms: *gravitas, gravity*

Fulvous golden-brown

Genre artistic category

Gloats brags about one's good fortune or about the misfortune of others. Synonyms: *boasts, swaggers*

Gossamer thin and very delicate cobwebs spun by small spiders, any substance that is very thin and delicate. Synonyms: *diaphanous, sheer, wispy*

Grandiloquence pompous speaking

Harangued aggressively pestered or criticized. Synonym: *berated*

Harebrained silly or foolish. Synonyms: *crackpot, ditzy, flaky, impracticable, madcap, rash, reckless, scatterbrained*

Harmonic relating to musical harmony. Synonyms: *dulcet, euphonic, mellifluous, melodious, polyphonic.* Antonyms: *cacophonous, dissonant*

Harmony notes combined to form a pleasant-sounding whole

Haste speed. Synonym: *expedition*

Haughty arrogant. Synonyms: *bombastic, pompous, supercilious*

Hedonism philosophy that advocates seeking pleasure

Heinous wicked or hated. Synonyms: *abhorrent, abominable, atrocious, baleful, contemptible,* *depraved, despicable, detestable, egregious, execrable, horrific, impious, iniquitous, loathsome, malevolent, monstrous, nefarious, odious, pernicious, reprehensible, unspeakable, villainous*

Histrionic overly dramatic

Homunculus miniature humanoid

Horde mob or tribe of *nomadic* (traveling) warriors. Synonym: *throng*

Hostilities fighting or aggression. Synonyms for hostility: *belligerence, truculence*

Hubris pride. Synonyms: *arrogance, conceit, egotism, haughtiness, hauteur, pomposity, superciliousness.* Antonym: *humility*

Hypothetical theoretical. Synonyms: *conjectural, notional, putative, speculative, supposed, suppositional*

Iambic using one unstressed syllable followed by one stressed syllable

Iambic pentameter a line of poetry with five pairs of unstressed and stressed syllables

Icon symbol. Synonym: *paragon*

Iconoclast one who attacks established beliefs

Iconography images associated with a style, the study of images and symbols

Ignoramus an ignorant person

Imminent happening soon. Synonyms: *forthcoming, impending, looming*

Immoderation excessiveness. Synonym: *intemperance*

Immortal unable to die

Immutable absolute or unchangeable. Synonym: *incontrovertible*

Imperious bossy, controlling, or domineering. Synonym: *peremptory*

Impertinent rude. Synonyms: *cheeky, contemptuous, contumelious, impudent, insolent, insubordinate, pert, sassy, saucy*

Impetuous spontaneous and impulsive. Synonyms: *hasty, heedless, imprudent, precipitate, rash, temerarious, unpremeditated*

Implicated involved, held responsible, or implied. Synonyms: *compromised, embroiled, enmeshed, ensnared, entangled, incriminated*

Implication indirect suggestion

Impotent powerless. Synonyms: *feeble, impuissant*

Impregnable unable to be broken into. Synonyms: *impenetrable, inviolable, invulnerable, unassailable*

Improbable unlikely. Synonyms: *absurd, dubious, fanciful, inconceivable*

Impudent rude. Synonyms: *cheeky, contemptuous, contumelious, impertinent, insolent, insubordinate, pert, sassy, saucy*

Impugn challenge

Impulsive spontaneous. Synonyms: *hasty, heedless, impetuous, imprudent, precipitate, rash, temerarious, unpremeditated*

In lieu of in place of

Inane silly or foolish. Synonyms: *absurd, asinine, fatuous, puerile, vacuous, vapid*

Inarticulately unclearly expressed. Synonyms: *incoherently, incomprehensibly, unintelligibly*

Inauspicious unlucky. Synonyms: *infelicitous, unfortunate, unpropitious*

Incendiary designed to cause fire or conflict. Synonyms: *combustible, flammable, seditious*

Inception starting point. Synonyms: *commencement, genesis, origin*

Incorrigible not able to be corrected or reformed. Synonyms: *inveterate, irredeemable*

Indictable able to be charged with a crime

Indifferent unconcerned or uncaring. Synonyms: *apathetic, cavalier, dismissive, dispassionate, impassive, insouciant, nonchalant, perfunctory.* Antonym: *solicitous (concerned)*

Indiscretions sinful or unwise actions. Synonyms for indiscretion: *impropriety, imprudence, injudiciousness, peccadillo, solecism, transgression*

Indispensable essential. Synonyms: *imperative, invaluable, requisite, vital.* Antonym: *superfluous (unnecessary)*

Inertia the tendency for things to continue along the path they are on

Inevitable unavoidable. Synonyms: *fated, ineluctable, ineludible, inexorable, predestined, predetermined*

Infirm weak. Synonyms: *debilitated, decrepit, feeble, frail*

Inherent natural or in-born. Synonyms: *innate, intrinsic*

Inhospitable harsh and unwelcoming. Synonyms: *austere, bleak, desolate, inimical, spartan, stark*

Innocuous harmless. Synonym: *benign*

Insatiable not able to be satisfied. Synonyms: *gluttonous, implacable, rapacious, ravenous, relentless, unappeasable, voracious*

Inscrutable difficult to understand. Synonyms: *abstruse, arcane, enigmatic, impenetrable, recondite*

Insipid flavorless, dull, and uninteresting. Synonyms: *banal, hackneyed, inane, jejune, lackluster, pedestrian, prosaic, trite, vacuous, vapid*

Insolent rude. Synonyms: *cheeky, contemptuous, contumelious, impertinent, impudent, insubordinate, pert, sassy, saucy*

Insufferable intolerable

Intact complete or undamaged

Intrepid fearless

Irksome annoying. Synonyms: *exasperating, galling, nettlesome, vexing*

Irrevocably irreversibly. Synonyms: *immutably, peremptorily.* Antonym: *temporarily*

Juvenile childish or immature. Synonyms: *puerile, sophomoric*

Keen sharp, penetrating, eager, intelligent

Kismet fate. Synonym: *providence*

Lapis deep blue. Synonym: *ultramarine*

Lark an unplanned or mischievous bit of amusement. Synonyms: *escapade, jape, prank, whim*

Liability problem, debt. Antonym: *asset*

Liaison agent or representative, secret love affair

Loathe hate. Synonyms: *abhor, condemn, despise, detest, disdain, execrate, scorn.* Antonym: *love*

Loquacious talkative. Synonyms: *effusive, expansive, garrulous, pleonastic, prolix, verbose, voluble.* Antonyms: *reticent, taciturn*

Luminary a person who "enlightens" and inspires others

Luminous radiant

Lycanthrope wolf-human

Macabre bloody, deathly, or gruesome. Synonyms: *ghastly, gory, morbid*

Majestic beautiful or dignified. Synonyms: *august, distinguished, noble, resplendent, stately, sumptuous*

Majesty dignity, power, or beauty

Malcontent troublemaker. Synonym: *dissident*

Malignant harmful

Malingering faking illness to avoid school or work

Mandate formal declaration. Synonyms: *decree, edict, fiat, proclamation*

Manifesto declaration of policy. Synonyms: *credo, creed, mission statement, platform*

Martinet strict disciplinarian. Synonyms: *doctrinaire, dogmatist, pedant, stickler*

Masochism the practice of liking and seeking pain

Matriarchy rule by women

Matriculate enroll in school

Maudlin overly sentimental or even self-pitying. Synonyms: *cloying, hokey, lachrymose, mawkish, mushy, saccharine, treacly*

Mawkish overly sentimental

Melancholy sad and gloomy. Synonyms: *atrabilious, desolate, disconsolate doleful, dolorous, dour, forlorn, lugubrious, morose, mournful, plaintive, woebegone, wretched.* Antonym: *cheerful*

Menace threat. Synonyms: *peril, plague*

Mercurial unpredictable or quickly changing. Synonyms: *capricious, erratic, fickle, fluctuating, impulsive, inconstant, labile, mutable, protean, temperamental, volatile, whimsical.* Antonym: *stable*

Merit earn, worthiness of praise. Synonym: *warrant*

Metaphor comparison

Miscreants villains. Synonyms: *malefactors, malfeasants, picaroons, reprobates, rogues, scoundrels*

Misogynist hater of women

Mitigated not complete

Modulation altering or changing, especially in music, from one key to another

Monarchy rule by a king or queen

Monogamous committed to one sexual partner

Morbid gruesome

Moribund lacking vitality or dying

Morose gloomy. Synonyms: *doleful, dour, glum, lugubrious, melancholic, morbid, sullen*

Mortal able to die

Mortified embarrassed. Synonyms: *abashed, chagrined, discomfited*

Multitudinous numerous. Synonyms: *abundant, copious, multifarious, myriad, profuse, prolific*

Munificent very generous. Synonyms: *beneficent, bounteous, bountiful, magnanimous, openhanded*

Nadir lowest point

Narcissism egotism. Synonyms: *solipsism, vanity*

Native home

Naught nothing

Necrophobia fear of death

Nefarious wicked. Synonyms: *baleful, depraved, heinous, impious, iniquitous, malevolent, pernicious*

Negotiate discuss terms for, find a way through. Synonyms: *arbitrate, compromise, conciliate, confer, debate, haggle, intercede, mediate, moderate, parley*

Neophytes beginners. Synonyms: *fledglings, initiates, novices, probationers, tenderfoots, tyros.* Antonym: *veterans*

Nepotism showing favoritism based on kinship or friendship

Nigh almost or near

Nihilist a person who rejects religion and believes that life is meaningless

Notorious well known for bad things. Synonym: *infamous*

Objective based on facts, rather than a person's own ideas

Obloquy harsh criticism

Obsequious excessively obedient or flattering. Synonyms: *fawning, ingratiating, oleaginous, servile, sycophantic, toady*

Obsolete outdated. Synonyms: *anachronistic, antediluvian, antiquated, archaic, bygone, defunct, démodé, extinct, outmoded, passé, superseded*

Obtuse slow to comprehend. Synonyms: *dense, thick*. Antonym: *astute*

Ocher golden-brown

Ogling staring with excessive or offensive sexual desire

Oligarchy rule by a small group of individuals

Ominous threatening. Synonyms: *foreboding, inauspicious, menacing*

Omnipotent all powerful

Omnipresent present all-over

Omniscient knowing everything

Opportunist a person who uses opportunities to his or her selfish advantage

Oppression cruel and unfair treatment. Synonyms: *despotism, persecution, repression, subjection, subjugation, suppression, tyranny*. Antonym: *freedom*

Oppressive harsh and constraining. Synonyms: *autocratic, despotic, dictatorial, draconian, repressive, tyrannical, undemocratic*. Antonyms: *humane, lenient*

Ossified hardened, rigid and resistant to change

Ostentatious a snobby, showy, or conceited display of wealth, especially in an attempt to impress. Synonyms: *pretentious, showy*

Overt obvious

Overtones subtle implications. Synonyms: *connotations, insinuations, intimations, nuances, undertones*

Pagan not Jewish or Christian

Panache flair. Synonym: *élan*

Pandemonium noisy disorder. Synonyms: *anarchy, bedlam, chaos, commotion, furor, hubbub, hullabaloo, mayhem, rumpus, tumult, turmoil, uproar*

Pandering giving in to the immoral desires of others

Paradox contradictory statement

Paramount of supreme importance. Synonyms: *foremost, key, predominant, primary*

Parity equality

Parley conference between opposing sides in a dispute

Parliament assembly of lawmakers

Parlously tremendously, dangerously

Pathetic pitiful

Patriarchal controlled by men

Patronize treat kindly but with a superior attitude, supporting or being a customer. Synonyms: *condescend, demean, denigrate*

Pedestrian ordinary and unimaginative, someone walking. Synonyms: *conventional, prosaic*

Pejorative critical

Penance self-punishment for having committed a wrong or sin. Synonyms: *amends, atonement, contrition, expiation*

Pensive thinking deeply. Synonyms: *brooding, contemplative, introspective, meditative, musing, reflective, ruminative*

Pentameter a line of poetry with five groups

Penurious poor or miserly. Synonym: *parsimonious*

Perfidious disloyal. Synonyms: *deceitful, duplicitous, traitorous, treacherous, treasonous*

Perilous dangerous

Perish become ruined or die

Pernicious destructive or wicked. Synonyms: *baleful, deleterious, detrimental, inimical, insidious, maleficent, malevolent, malignant, nefarious, noxious*. Antonym: *benevolent*

Petulant irritable. Synonyms: *cantankerous, churlish,*

curmudgeonly, fractious, irascible, peevish, querulous, sullen

Philanthropist one who loves humans and donates money to help charities

Philistine a person hostile to or ignorant of the arts and intellectual pursuits

Philosophy love of wisdom

Phobia fear

Pilgrimage religious or spiritual journey

Plausible reasonable, probable, or believable. Synonyms: *credible, feasible*. Antonyms: *implausible, incredible*

Plethoric excessive

Plutarchy rule by the wealthy

Poised calm and composed

Poltergeist disruptive ghost

Pompous arrogant. Synonyms: *affected, conceited, egotistic, haughty, pontifical, pretentious, sententious, supercilious, uppity, vain*

Poppysmic the sound of one's lips smacking

Pragmatic practical. Antonym: *idealistic*

Precipice cliff. Synonyms: *bluff, crag, escarpment, scarp*

Predator hunter

Preeminent greatest or most important. Synonyms: *foremost, illustrious, marquee, supreme*

Premeditated planned. Synonyms: *deliberate, intentional*

Prenuptially before marriage

Prestidigitation magic tricks. Synonym: *sleight of hand*

Presumptuous presuming too much—overly bold. Synonyms: *audacious, brazen, impertinent, impudent*

Pristine pure or perfect. Synonyms: *immaculate, intact*

Privy to in on or aware of. Synonym: *cognizant of*

Proclivity tendency

Prodigious enormous, amazing. Synonyms: *colossal, inordinate, mammoth, wondrous*

Prodigy genius. Synonyms: *mastermind, virtuoso, wunderkind*

Profusion abundance

Prognosis forecast or prediction

Proletariat working class. Synonyms: *hoi polloi, plebeians.* Antonym: *aristocracy*

Prologue introduction. Synonyms: *exordium, foreword, preamble, preface, prelude, proem.* Antonym: *epilogue*

Propagate spread. Synonyms: *breed, disseminate, proliferate, promulgate*

Propriety following the proper rules of behavior. Synonyms: *decorum, discretion, etiquette, protocol, punctilio, rectitude, refinement.* Antonym: *indecorum*

Prose ordinary writing

Prostrate lying face down on the ground

Prototype first model or typical example of something. Synonyms: *archetype, exemplar, paradigm, paragon, quintessence, template*

Providence fate, or the protective care of God. Synonym: *kismet*

Provincial narrow or unsophisticated. Synonyms: *insular, parochial.* Antonyms: *cosmopolitan, urbane*

Proximity nearness. Synonym: *propinquity*

Pugilist a boxer

Pugnacious quick to fight

Qualified able; not complete

Quidnunc a gossipy person

Ramifications consequences

Rampallion a scoundrel. Synonym: *fustilarian*

Rampant uncontrolled. Synonym: *unchecked*

Rapacious aggressively greedy. Synonyms: *acquisitive, avaricious, covetous, insatiable, mercenary, predatory.* Antonyms: *generous, munificent*

Reconcile settle or resolve

Reconciliatory settling, resolving, or making consistent

Redemption being saved, set free, or forgiven. Synonym: *absolution*

Reign rule; holding of an official title. Synonym: *incumbency*

Relentlessly constantly or tirelessly. Synonyms: *incessantly, inexorably, interminably, unremittingly*

Remorse regret for wrongdoing. Synonyms: *compunction, contrition, penitence, repentance, ruefulness*

Remorseless without regret. Synonyms: *callous, merciless, pitiless, ruthless*

Remote unlikely, far away

Rend tear apart. Synonyms: *sever, sunder, wrench*

Repressed put down or subdued. Synonyms: *oppressed, subjugated, tyrannized*

Repulsive disgusting. Synonyms: *abhorrent, abominable, execrable, ghastly, grotesque, hideous, horrendous, loathsome, noisome, noxious, repellent, repugnant, revolting, vile*

Resolute determined. Synonyms: *staunch, steadfast, unswerving*

Retribution revenge or punishment. Synonyms: *reprisal, requital, retaliation, retribution, vengeance*

Reverential with deep respect

Reveres deeply respects. Synonyms: *esteems, venerates*

Righteous moral. Synonym: *virtuous*

Righteousness morality. Synonyms: *rectitude, virtue.* Antonym: *vicefulness (immorality)*

Rigorous thorough, strict, demanding. Synonyms: *assiduous, conscientious, diligent, draconian, intransigent, meticulous, persnickety, punctilious, scrupulous, sedulous, stringent*

Rue regret. Synonyms for rueful: *contrite, penitent, remorseful, repentant*

Rural of the countryside, rather than the city. Synonyms: *bucolic, pastoral, rustic.* Antonym: *urban*

Sadist one who likes to inflict pain

Salvation being saved. Synonyms: *deliverance, redemption*

Samite a rich silk fabric used in the Middle Ages

Sanctuary a place or feeling of safety and comfort. Synonyms: *haven, refuge*

Savvy understand; practical, rather than theoretical, knowledge

Scholastic pertaining to school

Scintilla a tiny bit. Synonyms: *iota, modicum, particle*

Scruples concerns about being immoral. Synonyms: *compunctions, qualms*

Scrutiny close examination. Synonym: *probing*

Self-righteous with a superior attitude. Synonym: *sanctimonious*

Semblance appearance or similarity. Synonym: *resemblance*

Septic infected. Synonyms: *festering, purulent, putrefying, putrid, suppurating*

Serendipity a fortunate accident

Serene calm and peaceful. Synonyms: *equanimous, placid, poised (calm and composed), tranquil*

Servile overly obedient. Synonyms: *obsequious, sycophantic*

Sesquipedalianist a person who uses very long words

Shrew small mouse-like animal, bad-tempered woman. Synonyms: *termagant, virago*

Simile comparing two things by using the words "like" or "as"

Smite strike heavily, defeat

Sobriquet nickname

Solace comfort. Synonyms: *consolation, succor*

Solicitous concerned

Soliloquy speech where one thinks aloud, often alone. Synonyms: *aside, monologue*

Sporadic irregularly occurring. Synonyms: *desultory, erratic, intermittent*

Squalid dirty or immoral. Synonyms: *sordid, tawdry*

Squandered wasted

Star-crossed doomed

Subjective based on a person's own ideas

Subterranean underground

Subtext underlying theme or message

Summit highest point. Synonyms: *acme, apex, apogee, peak, pinnacle, zenith*. Antonym: *nadir*

Supercilious acting superior, arrogant

Superfluous unnecessary or more than needed. Synonym: *redundant*

Superstitious believing in supernatural causes and effects

Supplicant one who prays

Supreme highest

Surreptitious secret. Synonyms: *clandestine, covert, furtive*

Swag loot, a pretty wreath of flowers, or an ornamental curtain

Swarthy dark-skinned

Symbiotic mutually beneficial

Taciturn not talkative. Synonyms: *introverted, reserved, reticent*

Tactile relating to the sense of touch

Tantamount the same as, with the same effect as

Tawdry tasteless, vulgar, or immoral. Synonyms: *garish, gaudy*

Tawny golden-brown

Temerity bold rudeness. Synonyms: *audacity, chutzpah, effrontery, gall, impertinence, impudence, nerve, presumption*

Temperate mild. Synonym: *clement*

Tempestuous stormy, quick-tempered

Tenure term of office; assured employment. Synonym: *incumbency*

Titanic very large, strong, and powerful. Synonyms: *colossal, inordinate, mammoth, monumental, prodigious*

Tolerance leniency or open-mindedness. Synonyms: *forbearance, indulgence*

Topaz golden-brown

Tribute something that honors. Synonyms: *homage, paean*

Trifling unimportant. Synonyms: *exiguous, incidental, negligible, nominal, nugatory, pettifogging, petty, trivial*

Truncated shortened. Synonyms: *abbreviated, curtailed*

Tumescent swollen; pompous language. Synonyms: *distended, engorged, tumid, turgid*

Turgid swollen; pompous language. Synonyms: *distended, engorged, tumescent, tumid*

Turquoise greenish-blue. Synonym: *aquamarine*

Tyros beginners. Synonyms: *fledglings, initiates, neophytes, novices, probationers, tenderfoots.* Antonym: *veterans*

Unconditionally completely

Uncouth lacking polite manners. Synonyms: *boorish, indecorous, loutish, plebeian, unrefined*

Undulating moving in a flowing, wavelike motion

Unequivocal definite. Synonyms: *categorical, incontrovertible, indubitable, unconditional, unqualified*

Unfathomable impossible to understand. Synonyms: *enigmatic, impenetrable, inscrutable*

Universal all-inclusive. Synonyms: *omnipresent, ubiquitous*

Unmitigated complete. Synonyms: *absolute, categorical, consummate, unconditional, unequivocal, unqualified, untempered*

Unrequited not returned. Synonym: *unreciprocated*

Unruly undisciplined or disorderly. Synonyms: *boisterous, contumacious, disobedient, intractable, irrepressible, obstreperous, rambunctious, recalcitrant, refractory, restive, willful*

Untoward inconvenient, inappropriate. Synonyms: *improper, infelicitous, malapropos*

Unyielding stubborn, unbending, or determined. Synonyms: *dogged, intractable, intransigent, obdurate, obstinate, pertinacious, tenacious*

Utility usefulness. Synonyms: *efficacy, productiveness*

Vacuous mindless or empty. Synonyms: *fatuous, inane, insipid, vacant, vapid.* Antonym: *intelligent*

Valiant brave. Synonyms: *audacious, dauntless, doughty, gallant, indomitable, intrepid, lionhearted, valorous.* Antonym: *cowardly*

Vapid dull and ordinary. Synonyms: *hackneyed, insipid, jejune, lackluster, pedestrian, trite, vacuous*

Veers turns suddenly

Vengeance revenge. Synonyms: *reprisal, requital, retaliation, vindication*

Verbiage long-winded speaking or writing. Synonyms: *circumlocution, loquacity, periphrasis, prolixity, superfluity, verbosity, wordiness*

Veracity truthfulness

Verbose long-winded. Synonyms: *chatty, effusive, garrulous, loquacious, pleonastic, prolix, voluble*

Verify confirm

Verily truly

Verisimilitude the appearance of seeming real

Verity a fundamental truth

Vestal virgin or a pure and chaste (nonsexual) person

Viable possible. Synonym: *feasible*

Vices immoral behaviors. Synonyms: *corruption, debauchery, decadence, degeneracy, depravity, dissipation, dissolution, iniquity, lechery, perversion, transgression, trespass, turpitude, villainy*

Vichyssoise a chilled soup of potatoes, leeks, and cream

Vile disgusting or evil

Vindictive revengeful. Synonyms: *malevolent, malicious, rancorous, spiteful, vengeful*

Virtue good quality. Synonyms: *rectitude, righteousness*

Viscosity gooeyness. Synonyms for viscous: *gelatinous, glutinous, mucilaginous, mucoid, mucous, treacly, viscid, viscoelastic*

Viscous gooey

Voluminous plentiful. Synonyms: *abundant, bounteous, capacious, commodious, prodigious, profuse, prolific*

Ward person looked after or protected by another

Wretch unhappy or wicked person. Synonyms: *miscreant, picaroon, reprobate, rogue, scoundrel*

Xenophile one who loves or is interested in foreign people, ideas, and objects

Xenophobic afraid of foreigners

Yoke burden, connection, or harness. Synonyms: *bondage, bonds, chains, domination, enslavement, fetters, hegemony, oppression, servitude, shackles, subjection, subjugation, thrall, tyranny*

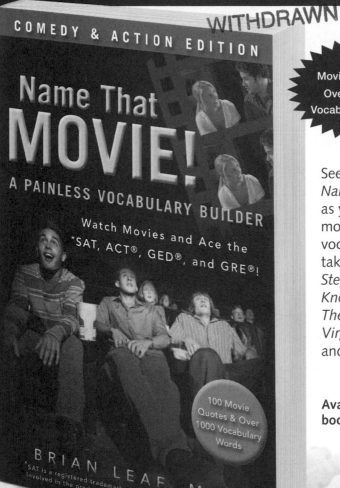